The
Morn's
The
Fair

By
William Fyfe Hendrie

This book is dedicated to

Gordon,
Jean,
Lindsay
and Andrew

from whom I have received far more than my "fair" share of hospitality.

"The Morn's The Fair" first printed and published in June, 1982.

ISBN 0 9507156 1 1

Also by the same author
"Bo'ness, Three Hundred Years"
"West Lothian Lore"
"Forth to the Sea"
and with James McCue *"Alice in Wonderland"*, a dramatised version of Lewis Carroll's famous children's classic published by MacMillan Education Ltd.

Acknowledgements
Cover and illustrations—Scott Guthrie Pollock
Bo'ness Fair photographs—John Doherty
Other photos West Lothian District Library, Sandy Paris and James Nimmo
Proofs—Charles A. H. Grant
and others

Printed by S.K.I. Graphics (Scotland) Ltd., 45 St Marnock Street, Bridgeton, Glasgow

Contents

Chapter 1

Bo'ness Fair

THE MORN'S THE FAIR
"The morn's the fair, and I'll be there,
and I'll hae up ma curly hair.
I'll meet ma lad at the fit o' the stair,
an' I'll gie him a dram and a wee drap mair."

These are the lines which the lassies of Bo'ness used to chant every year on the second Thursday in July, as they raced down the steep slopes of the School Brae, Castleloan Brae and Cowdenhill Brae. For this Thursday in July was both the Fair E'en, the day before Bo'ness Fair and the day they escaped from the dominie and his tawse for the seven long glorious weeks of the summer holidays.

In a way their simple rhyme captures all the magic and anticipated excitement, for the Fair was indeed the highlight of the year for the bairns of Bo'ness, while at the same time owing its origin to, "a dram and a wee drap mair."

For while today to Bo'nessians, Bo'ness without its Fair would seem inconceivable as Bo'ness without the River Forth or Bo'ness without its braes, yet at one time no self respecting person would have anything to do with this annual event, which is now the largest and most spectacular of its kind in the country. Unlike most of Scotland's summer celebrations in towns throughout the Borders and Lowlands, which can trace origins to the traditional riding of the marches ceremonies or to old castle fairs, Bo'ness Fair began, as one witness of the time described it, "as a drunken orgy" among the coalminers of the district.

Until the latter part of the 18th century it was customary for all Scottish miners to be thirled, that is bound to their pits, as were any children who were born to them while they worked in them. Thus the bondage was continued from generation to generation and if any of the miners tried to escape from this virtual slavery the colliery masters had the power to send their overseers to drag them back to punish them severely. Even when a colliery owner sold his pit, the miners were included as part of the transaction. At last, in 1774, a law was passed forbidding the thirling of miners and their families to the coal pits, but those already tied to the mines were not granted their freedom straightaway and it was not until 1799 that an'Act declared that, "all the colliers in that part of Great Britain called Scotland, are hereby declared to be free from their servitude."

It was to celebrate this new found liberty that the miners of Bo'ness, who formed a very closeknit community of their own, staged their first Fair. From then on the Fair was held every year on the Friday in July which fell between the 12th and the 19th, a date already connected with one of the four feeing fairs for which Anne, Duchess of Hamilton gained parliamentary permission shortly after she won her battle for burgh status for Bo'ness in 1668.

On this their only holiday in the whole year all the pit workers from the long, low miners' rows at Borrowstoun and Newtown, marched down to the narrow winding streets of Bo'ness and on out through Corbiehall to Kinneil house, home of the Duke of Hamilton, who owned many of the local pits. In front of the big house, on its hilltop overlooking the River Forth, the miners led by their elected Deacon, wearing his ornate bonnet, sash and sword, were received by the Duke's estate factor, who provided them all with glasses of whisky toddy.

From Kinneil the march continued, with frequent halts for refreshments, to the old Grange, the house of the other big colliery owner in Bo'ness, Mr James John Cadell. Mr Cadell, himself, always welcomed his men and on this one day in the year it is reported that the "Maister" relaxed his usual severe manner and even handed round the glasses of whisky toddy to his miners, an act which greatly delighted them. A brass band, imported during the early years from Falkirk, always accompanied the marchers and while they enjoyed their free drinks, it played on the lawn in front of the old Grange, before leading them down to the banks of the Forth, where the horse races were held on the foreshore, throughout the afternoon.

The most distinguished visitor to the Bo'ness races was Robert Burns, but he was as little impressed with the standard of the races as he was with the rest of Bo'ness, which he described as, "that dirty ugly place, Borrowstounness", and which certainly did not inspire him to verse. It is little wonder that Burns was not inspired by the races, for the mounts were just local carriage and waggon horses, pressed into service for the day and generally most of them had already done duty earlier in the day, carrying the Deacon and other miner's leaders at the head of the procession.

Once the last race was over the crowd returned to Corbiehall, where the booths and the side stalls of the fairground were set up and the gingerbread sellers did a roaring trade. Later there was dancing in the Town Hall' where all the miners and their wives and daughters could afford to join in the merrymaking, as they paid separately for each dance at one penny a time.

Drinking, was however, the main attraction of the Fair and the town's many pubs and inns were crowded. In those days there were no licensing laws and the pubs stayed open throughout the night so that the festivities continued right into the following Saturday or at least as long as the miner's money lasted. The remainder of the weekend the miners spent sobering up, returning to the pits to start work again early on the Monday morning. Their annual holiday was over and there was only the next year to look forward to, to brighten their dreary existence, so they immediately appointed a new Deacon to act as their leader and make a start to the arrangements for the following year's Fair.

Gradually as the years of Queen Victoria's long reign passed and the barriers between the coal miners and the other members of the community were slowly broken down, other workers in the town began to take part in the Fair and each of the trades found in Bo'ness was represented in the procession. One of the most interesting and colourful groups in the procession was that made up by the craftsmen from the local potteries, for the potters always wore their white trousers, white aprons tied with black ribbons, black tail coats and tall black lum hats and carried with them examples of their craft and symbols of their trade including model china sailing ships, and minature kilns.

Although for a time more of the townsfolk took part in the festivities, as Queen Victoria's reign wore on the Fair's popularity began to wane partly because of the excessive drinking which took place at it and which shocked the more soberly minded citizens.

Finally, in 1894, the miners realised that something had to be done if their annual celebration was not to die out and so they approached the local Police Commissioners, who at that time governed Bo'ness, before the creation of a Town Council, and suggested that these gentlemen should take part in the Fair Procession. The very proposal caused consternation in the town and several of the Commissioners were opposed to associating themselves in any way with this day of drinking, one demanding to know whether they would be expected, "to get fou like the rest?" After long and heated discussions, however, Provost Ballantine persuaded his colleagues to join in the proceedings, on the strict understanding that they would be properly conducted.

Announcing their decision, Provost Ballantine stated grandly that he felt that, "it became the authorities of any place that, for one day at least, they should be on a level with their neighbours", and that therefore it was, "quite in keeping that the Commissioners of Bo'ness and others outside should for a few hours, join in the general friendship and forget any differences that have taken place."

And so that year the parade was led as usual by the miner's Deacon, but he was followed by the Provost and the Commissioners in open landaux, flanked by scarlet coated outriders and led by banner bearers proudly carrying a large banner depicting the Burgh Coat of Arms with its ship under full sail and on a scroll beneath it the town's motto "sine Metu", "Without Fear".

At last a touch of pageantry had been added to the Bo'ness Fair, but this was nothing compared to what was to come only three years later in 1897 at the time of Queen Victoria's Diamond Jubilee, for the wave of celebrations, which swept across the country was seized by Provost Stewart as the ideal opportunity to bring the children of the town into the festivities for the first time. As his model he chose Lanark's Lanimer Day, at which the boys and girls of the town elected one of their school friends to be their Fair Queen. The new style Bo'ness Fair was received with great enthusiasm by the local people and the first school girl 'Queen', Grace Strachan, chosen by the pupils of the old Anderson Academy, was cheered as she rode in her carriage in the first grand procession after her coronation, which was performed in Craigallen Park by Mrs Balfour, wife of the chairman of Bo'ness School Board.

From Craigallan the procession made its way out to the Kinnigars Park at Carriden, where the first Queen's revels were held. The route took it down the new Philpingstone Road, which was officially declared open by Mrs Cadell, before the Queen's horse drawn carriage entered it from Grange Terrace.

In all over 2000 children from Bo'ness Infant School, Grangepans Infant School, Bo'ness Public School, Kinneil School, Borrowstoun School and Carriden School as well as the Anderson Academy, took part in the first Fair. As well as Queen Grace, many of her classmates from the Old Academy and boys and girls from all the other schools played the parts of gaily dressed lords and ladies of the royal court and fairies flower girls and other characters, just as their grandchildren and great grandchildren still do every summer.

One well known Bo'nessian who had vivid memories of that first Children's Fair Festival was the late Findlay MacGillivray, and at the age of well over 90 he took a few minutes off from looking after his famous collection of cage birds, to look back and tell me about it.

"It was a really beautiful day, and she was a real bonnie Queen, but it's the procession I remember best," he told me as we sat on a bench in his aviary. 'Just as in the old miner's march," he continued, "all the trades in the town were represented in the procession. Biggest favourites with the children were the wee pit ponies, which were brought up specially from the pit bottom. The miners were very proud of their ponies, which were beautifully groomed for this the only time in the whole year that they ever saw daylight.

"After they had clipped-clopped by, came five horse-drawn decorated lorries entered by the five foundries in the town. Each vied with the other to display the most intricate examples of their

SGP 1982

9

craft and on each were pattern makers, actually at work. The potters also worked on their two lorries, which were decorated with model sailing ships, wally dugs, and other china ornaments, made and painted by them.

"Even the local football and cricket teams entered that first procession, all mounted on horses hired from the neighbouring farms like the Gauze, the Drum and North Bank. I wasn't happy at all about this for I knew very well that these lads, who included my brother, knew very little about riding, and of course the cheering of the crowd, their own showing off and the steepness of the braes between Craigallan and Kinnigars Park at Carriden where the first Queen's revels were held, all combined to make it more and more difficult for them to keep control of their mounts. My worst fears were realised when suddenly my brother's horse bolted and cannoned into one of the ladies watching the procession go past. By a miracle she was not injured, but her new Fair dress was ruined and my brother had to pay for it, which made it a very costly first Fair for him."

The following year the Queen was again chosen from the Anderson Academy, but then it was decided that each school in the town should take it in turn to provide the Queen and her retinue, a custom which has continued ever since, and so in 1899 little Borrowstoun School chose Lizzie McDonald to be it's first Queen. It was as a pupil of Borrowstoun School that well remembered Bo'ness school teacher, the late Miss Grace Livingston, first went to the Fair, and as she trained later generations of pupils at Bo'ness Public School for their parts in the big day, she often laughingly recalled her picture of herself on her first Fair morning. "Like every other little girl I wore a white Fair frock, and like every other child, girls as well as boys, I wore a school cap. Each school had its own distinctive colour of cap and for Borrowstoun it had to be blue and white. Well do I remember my mother's search for a cap big enough for my head, but they simply did not make school caps in size 7 and 7/8s and so I just had to wear what she could get perched high on top of my bushy hair. It was of course no protection against the broiling sun as we marched from the school down through Newtown to the Glebe Park then all the way to Castleloan for the sports, not to mention walking all the way home again in the afternoon. At the end of the day I remember suffering agonies with a face and neck burned to a brilliant terra-cotta by the sun and the bliss of mother's old-fashioned cure of buttermilk and baking-soda."

Four years later it was again Borrowstoun's turn to pick the Queen, and Queen Christina Blackwood had little Grace Livingston in her retinue as her Queen of the Fairies, but only after a protest as Miss

Livingston loved to remember. "When I heard the result of the voting I immediately said, 'But what about my poor feet?' for there were no hurls for fairies in those days. One of my classmates who was much keener on the idea than I was immediately offered to go to the Headmaster and tell him that she would take my place. Within seconds she was back. 'The Maister says YOU'LL WALK', she reported, and that was the end of my Fair rebellion. Walk I did, and looking back on that Fair Day I always recall the story of the little Glasgow pupil who, on being asked by his teacher how he knew when summer had come, replied at once, 'By the tar bilin' up in the streets.' Well, the tar fairly 'biled' on that Fair Day, for it was a real scorcher, and my most vivid memory of it is of Miss Duguid, Grange School's Infant Mistress, wrenching one unfortunate wee girl from the tarry moorings in Corbiehall in which she had become firmly embeded during one of the long halts in the procession."

While Miss Livingston's memories of Borrowstoun Fairs were all sweltering July days, Bo'ness Public School was not nearly so lucky when it came its turn to choose its Queen in 1906. That first Public Queen was Jane Grant, who later became Mrs J. Jones of Maidenpark, and she remembers wakening on the morning of the big day.

"My mother told me as soon as I woke up that it was raining, but of course I kept on hoping that it would go off. All morning however, it got heavier and

11

heavier, and by 11 o'clock it was simply lashing down, and so I became the only Queen to have her coronation in the Town Hall. Everyone was so kind to me and said how pretty it all looked under the lights."

Fortunately the following year the sun did shine again and Mrs Jones was able to wear her beautiful flowered bonnet and carry a parasol, when she surrendered her crown as ex-Queen to Queen Mary Duffy of St Mary's School. Queen Mary was St Mary's first Queen and with its participation in the festivities the list of schools was almost complete. Only Grange remained to be opened and it was several years before its turn came round to choose Ina Ritchie as its first Queen in 1911.

The opening of the new Grange School meant that older pupils stopped attending Carriden and so after choosing only two Queens, Margaret Easton in 1901 and Margaret Allen in 1905, it disappeared from the list of schools. Just as Grange School took over Carriden's senior pupils so it in turn lost its secondary pupils when all secondary schooling in Bo'ness was centralised at the new Academy when it opened in 1931. Next year the Academy pupils chose Helen Burnett to be their first Queen from the new school in Academy Road, and Grange School from then on chose its Fair characters including its last pre-war Queen, Andrea Walker, from amongst its remaining primary pupils.

The 1930's brought changes in the educational scene not just at the Grange and the Academy, but also at the Public and Borrowstoun. For as the Public took over the old Academy building overlooking the Forth it now had room to accommodate Borrowstoun's dwindling roll of older pupils and Borrowstoun chose its last Queen, Margaret McMahon, 1933.

From then on, with the exception of the war years, the regular roll of Kinneil, Grange, Public, St Mary's, and the Academy has been used to select the Queen, until Deanburn Primary chose 11 year old Linda Dow as its first Queen in 1974.

As is but appropriate, the local miners whose ancestors started it all, still play a big part in the festivities and they are the acknowledged experts in the art of building the huge decorative arches, which span the roads in front of the homes of the Queen and her Chief Lady in Waiting, the first street spanning arch being erected in 1905. It was built by the miners who lived in Snab Rows and among the moving spirits responsible for it were the late Tom Brodie and Mr Charlie Young, who now lives in Maidenpark. Weeks of work went into the construction of the huge wooden frames but it was completed and decked

12

BO'NESS & CARRIDEN PRIZE BAND.

Bo'ness and Carriden Band pose with colliery owner Henry Mowbray Cadell in front of his home "The Grange"

One of the decorated vehicles in the procession at Bo'ness Fair.

the rain of the previous week. He had got the ferns, however, so I stayed on just a wee while longer to fix them on."

"There wasn't much of the night left when I finally got home after 6 o'clock, and you can imagine the row from my young bride, especially when I told her that I had to be out again by half past to help Mr White, the undertaker, put up the decorations in the Glebe Park."

That new bride of 47 years ago certainly learned to live with her husband's other love for arches, for she now recalls how, even when she enjoyed a Saturday night out during the weeks before the Fair, the crepe paper went too so that no time was wasted making the thousands of paper roses needed for his prize creations.

The use of paper roses, papier mache, stone effect wallpaper and all the other modern aids to arch building are, of course, a reminder of the ever-increasing difficulty of finding adequate supplies of boxwood. This Mr Heath claims dates back to 1930 when a particularly large arch was erected at Richmond Cross Roads for Queen Kathleen Jamieson. George Clark, Balfour Patton and George Sneddon are some of the names which Mr Heath recalls in connection with the monster arch, 60 feet wide and 33 feet high, which spanned Linlithgow Road and which robbed Kinneil Woods of all its boxwood.

From then on arch builders had to go as far away as Perth to ensure sufficient supplies and although large green arches did continue into the years after the Second World War with a particularly fine one erected at Cadzow Avenue for Queen Mary Sneddon in 1947, the days of the traditional arch were clearly numbered when the first of the turreted style arches was successfully built across Philpingston Road in 1951, the year Grange School pupil Margaret Henderson was Queen.

Like most old-timers Mr Heath has his reservations about the use of modern materials in arch building, but to find out what today's judges look for in the annual competition, I asked local artist Guthrie Pollock, who accompanied by John Cannon and Mrs F. R. S. Marr from Edinburgh, spends most of each Fair morning performing this tricky task.

"Simplicity of design, novelty value and good finish all count," Mr Pollock told me. "When we drive up on a Fair morning an arch often looks good from a distance but when we look more carefully and go round the back, it is often less impressive," he continued.

As an art teacher Mr Pollock admits that he also looks for good use of colour and prefers decorations to be under, rather than overdone.

16

"There is a terrible temptation to put on everything but the kitchen sink," he added "and especially on small arches this can be disastrous. At the other end of the scale some arches now have scarcely any decor at all as they rely so much on special lighting effects, which look wonderful by night, but which are difficult to judge when we see them in daylight in the morning".

Mr Pollock also feels that the layout of many of the newest areas of the town make it difficult to give the small arches as much appearance as they deserve as they are so often hidden away round corners and in cul-de-sacs, which makes it difficult even for the judges to find them.

To complete their arches in time for the judges tour of inspection early on the Fair morning, many of the builders work throughout the night as do the other enthusiasts busy putting the finishing touches to the elaborate tableaux and decorated floats, which are always a highlight of the mile long grand procession. Great rivalry exists among the tableaux builders and details are always kept as close a secret as possible until the big floats emerge on the Fair morning to make their slow way to the Chance Park for the judging ceremony.

The decorated lorries of today's Fair keep alive a link with the old miners' Fair for in their procession the rear was always brought up by the local carters with their carts and horses gaily decorated for the occasion. Today horses, apart from the Champion's mount, have disappeared from the procession, but the old Bo'ness comment, "She's all dressed up like a Fair horse" is still occasionally heard.

Tradition is also maintained in the coronation ceremony, which has changed very little over the years. Apart from the shortening of the original Herald's proclamation and the increased importance of the young presentees in fact the only major change from the ceremony at which Queen Grace Strachan was crowned has been the introduction of the now famous Fair songs. In the very earliest of the Children's Fairs the songs were always "Scots Wha Hae", "Three cheers of the Red, White and Blue" and "Auld Lang Syne". The first of our present Fair songs "Our Festal Day", by Mr R. Fleming, set to music by Mr F. C. Schofield and it proved so popular that a few years later in 1903, "Hail to our Queen", by Mr Hope A. Thomson with music by Mr L. Dyer Appleby, was added to the proceedings. Over the last sixty years these two songs have become very dear to the hearts of Bo'nessians and they have been sung wherever they meet, even at Hampden Park, Glasgow, when Bo'ness United won the final of the Scottish Junior Cup. The words are as follows:

> See the summer sun is gleaming
> Shining bright o'er land and sea,
> Nature's face with smiles is beaming
>   Symbol of festivity.
> All the earth is gay and gaudy,
> Mirth and joy together stray,
> Bright Sol lendeth all his glory,
>   To illume our Festal Day.
>   Hail! Hail! Hail!
> With a laugh loud and long,
> With a dance and a song,
> We hail our Festal Day.

Woods have donn'd their fairest garments,
Flowers refreshed with morning dew,
Brighten sylvan nook and valley
    With the beauty of their hue.
Hill and upland, green and golden,
Where the whin and broom hold sway,
Echo back the gladsome chorus
    Hail! All hail our Festal Day.
        Hail! Hail! Hail!
With a laugh loud and long.
With a dance and a song
We hail our Festal Day.

   Words by the late R. Fleming   *Music by E. C. Schofield*

We hail our chosen Queen today
To her our humble homage pay,
While music swells mid banners gay,
And sunbeams guild the scene,
Her faithful subjects see her crowned,
With all her lords and ladies round,
And then our happy shouts resound,
All hail our chosen Queen.
        Chorus
Hail! Hail our Queen today
Hail! Hail! our chosen Queen
Now raise your voices with a cheer
Hurrah! for our Queen.
We crown her with a crown of gold
Then with her train and guards so bold,
We march to some fair field to hold,
The Royal Revels there
Where wild birds sing and daisies grow,
We'll romp and bright as they, we'll show
A field of living flowers that grow
With life devoid of care.
Hail! Hail! our Queen today, etc.

   Words by A. Thomson   *Music by L. Dyer Appleby*

20

To begin with the new Fair songs were always played by a quartette made up of "Baker's Rab" Robert Sneddon, W. Robertson, D. Sneddon and that grand old man of Kinneil Band, T. Gow Robertson. Now they are played by either the full Kinneil or Carriden Bands, which along with seven other pipe or brass bands play such a big part in the Fair, from the moment they start the big day by parading through the streets of the town, until the final moments of the Queen's revels, now held in the Douglas Park.

The importance of the bands in the Fair proceedings has now been recognised by the introduction into the festivities of an open brass band contest which attracts leading bands from all over Scotland. Music from even further afield has been introduced by the invitation to the Fair of overseas school bands, singers and dancers from Norway, Russia, Poland and Canada. The inclusion of these international groups is typical of the new enthusiasm which has brought a new sparkle to the Fair during the last few years. Now the full range of Fair activities includes the Kirkin' of the Queen Ceremony, school sports tournaments, the open air brass band contest, and a torchlight procession on the Fair E'en.

The Fair proceedings themselves have taken on a new glitter thanks to the provision of a new crown, sceptre and robes all made by top Scottish craftsmen and bought as a result of the tremendous respose to a local appeal. A new glamour has also come to the grand procession with the introduction of continental style tableaux for the Queen, her retinue and the fairies and flower girls, to complete the modern image the revels have now been transformed into a spectacular Royal Command Performance. For over two hours Scotland's foremost stage and television personalities appear before our Fair Queen and an audience of over 20,000 people.

It is in this atmosphere that each summer's Fair takes place and as the sound of over 3,000 school children singing "Our Festal Day" rises high above the River Forth, everyone of the huge crowd assembled in the Glebe Park knows that yet another Fair is nearing its climax. As the hands of the big Town Hall clock move steadily towards 11 o'clock, the boy champion issues his traditional challenge, "If anyone here shall deny the Queen's title to the throne, I am here, ready to defend it, in single combat". Then exactly as the hour chimes out the Queen is crowned; the moment for which she has trained for over three months has arrived; the moment which she will never forget, for she knows that on this summer Friday morning her home town has paid her what has become its highest honour.

Chapter 2

Fair Memories

"Elizabeth Sneddon, youngest daughter of Mr and Mrs William Sneddon, James Place, has been by the popular vote of the senior pupils of Kinneil School, appointed school Queen."

So announced the "Linlithgowshire Gazette" on Friday 28th May 1920.

After four years of war the Fair had been revived in July 1919 and in 1920 there was tremendous enthusiasm in the town to make the second post war Fair even more successful than the first. Would it be possible to reintroduce the school caps, which had been such a colourful feature of the Fairs before the war, but which had not been available in 1919 due to post war shortages? Would there be enough material to allow the fairies, who had been absent from the 1919 Fair, to return to the scene? These were two of the questions discussed at length at the Fair Committee meetings. Other matters hotly debated that year seem strangely reminiscent of those of the present day. There were difficulties over catering, while councillor Angus Livingston was vigourously campaigning for a shorter route. In the end it was agreed to keep the same route as the previous year with procession going round the town, along Corbiehall and up the Snab Brae to the Ladywell Park with the coronation ceremony taking place here after the procession.

By the summer of 1920 most of the menfolk from Bo'ness had returned from the army and as May gave way to June the Fair Committee urged them to build arches all along the procession route. Many of them certainly had plenty of time to do so, for strikes were widespread in the town as the former soldiers discovered that the brave new world which they had fought for was not so wonderful after all. In the pits especially, there was a great deal of unrest as British coal fought to regain markets lost during the war. One group of Bo'ness miners from the Cadell's pits were in fact to miss the Fair of 1920 as they spent the whole summer hundreds of miles from home beyond the Arctic Circle at Spitsbergen, trying to find a new cheap source of coal for the Scottish Spitsbergen Syndicate.

In Bo'ness, one group of workers for whom there was more than ample work were the shipbreakers and with the battleship H.M.S. Exmouth, a cruiser, a whole fleet of submarines and many small naval vessels all redundant after the war, queuing to be scrapped at Bridgeness and Carriden, one colourful side effect as far as the Fair was concerned was the abundance of ships' bunting and signal flags available to decorate the whole town.

Even the front of the stage in the Town Hall was bedecked with flags for the Academy end of term prize giving at which Margaret Park received the Stewart Gold Medal, Louisa Begg the Stewart Silver Medal, Howard L Pritchard the prize as dux of the 5th year and Mary Baptie the prize as dux of the 4th year. Earlier the audience had been entertained to a performance of "The Tempest", in which leading roles were played by Helen McLellan and Betty Watt.

As the audience of parents and friends left the Town Hall many of them must have wondered if the Academy's stage effects for "The Tempest" had not been a bit too realistic for they were met by a downpour of rain and a cold wind blowing up from the river, which made it feel more like November than July. Rain had in fact had been the main feature of the weather since the month began and when it was still wet the following morning even those in Bo'ness who steadfastly believed the local tradition that the Fair always got the same weather as Linlithgow Marches, must have begun to doubt if they could really hope for the brilliant sunshine which their neighbours across the hills had enjoyed in June.

Friday 16th July 1920 did however dawn fair and by the time that the children began to gather at their schools to receive their buns and bananas the sun was shining. By eleven o'clock the procession was already marshalled at the East Partings and as the old Town Clock chimed out the hour it moved off along South Street.

"The thing I remember most," recalled the chief lady in waiting at that Fair, Annie Queenan, the late Mrs T, Pettigrew of Philipstoun Road, "were the crowds who lined the route." And the crowds were certainly not disappointed for the 1920 procession showed no sign of the post war shortages which had affected the 1919 Fair. Back were the open landeaux which had not been available the previous year due to a shortage of horses. Back were the traditional school caps, the red white and blue ones worn by the Kinneil pupils, both boys and girls, receiving special cheers from the crowds. And back too were the fairies and in addition there was the extra spectacle of the little "May Blossoms".

Especially popular with the crowds was the Grange School's contribution to the procession, "Little Bow Peep" for young Helen Pow had a real live sheep to look after as she rode through the streets on the horse drawn float designed and decorated by Topping Neilson of Bo'ness Co-operative Society. Other presentees that year included "Gypsy Boy and Girl" from the public, "Japanese Lady and Gentleman" from St Mary's, "Powder Puff" and "Jester" from Kinneil, "Cinderella" from the Infant School in South Street, "Scots Guard Officer in full regimentals", from Borrowstoun, "Bubbles and Dolly Varden" from Carriden and "Bonnie Prince Charlie and Flora McDonald" from Blackness.

Out past the merry-go-rounds and side stalls in Corbiehall the procession led by Bo'ness Pipe Band made its way west with the fact that it was a Kinneil Fair becoming even clearer with the decorations increasing steadily until that year's highlight the great arch at the Snab was finally reached. Built by the miners at Kinneil pit it was said to be the finest arch ever seen in the town and certainly with its main span surmounted by a crown and two smaller arches across the pavements it was one of the largest seen up until that time.

24

The steep brae from the Snab up to the Ladywell Park produced a slight hitch in the proceedings when the driver in charge of Ballantine's Grange Foundry float decided that his horse was too warm to tackle the hill without a rest. The short pause was equally welcomed by the human participants in the procession who were refreshed by the inhabitants of the miners rows who quickly fetched pitchers of water for the children and perhaps something slightly stronger for the bandsmen, from their spick and span homes which were all freshly painted and whitewashed for the occasion.

Once the procession was underway again it did not take long to reach the park where Mrs Gladstone, wife of the late rector of the Academy, was waiting to crown the Queen. According to the "Gazette's" reporter Queen Elizabeth was, "a tall fine complexioned girl who carried her honours with regal dignity and who looked lovely in a three quarter length dress of cream crepe de chene."

"Never had the park held such a vast throng and never had the crowning ceremony been so varied and rich in colour. The sun shone as Queen Elizabeth received all the young presentees, but just as the stage was cleared a sinister change took place in the weather and soon the first drops of rain were felt."

The "Gazette" report goes on to describe how the Queen and her retinue were rushed to shelter in Kinneil House, how the Maypole dancers defied the weather and how the bands played on, but most of the spectators soon set off for home to enjoy the traditional Fair meal of steak pie. For many Bo'ness families that year steak pie was something of a luxury, because meat prices had recently soared to such unprecedented heights that an emergency meeting under the chairmanship of Mr Robert Baptie had been held in the town only the week before as a result of which the local butchers led by Mr McMinn had accused the Scottish Farmers of outright profiteering. In July 1920 one butcher's shop in South Street was for the first time selling imported frozen meat at much lower prices, but it was looked upon with deep suspicion and was certainly not considered good enough to be included in the Fair steak pies.

In the evening the rain continued to fall, no doubt encouraging many to go to the pictures rather than the shows. Mr Jeffrey's "Picture House" was considered to have a very strong bill with Charlie Chaplin in "His Generation" and episode seven of "Lightning Bryce", but the following week Louis Dickson's establishment was expected to draw the crowds when it presented the Fair film, produced and directed by Mr Dickson himself.

For those who prefered to spend the evening in the Anchor Tavern, or one of the many other local pubs, there was little chance of the Fair night becoming the drunken orgy of Victorian times, because closing time was at 9 p.m. prompt, and next day there was the further disappointment when at the very last minute the local publicans all decided not to take up the Bo'ness magistrates offer to allow them to open specially from noon until four o'clock in addition to the usual six till nine opening.

On that Saturday in any case many Bo'nessians left the town, 369 travelling by train to Edinburgh, and 142 to Glasgow, while Mr Boyd's two new open topped char-a-bancs both carried full compliments to Loch Lomond. Apart from the day trippers, the boyscouts of St Andrew's Church under scoutmaster McIntosh and the Craigmaillan scouts under Mr Richard Sheddon set out for their annual camp at Longniddry, and several families departed to enjoy a week at the seaside at Rothesay, North Berwick and Arbroath. As they relaxed in their deck chairs perhaps some of the grown ups read copies of Fred Sleath's new book, "Breaker of Ships". Unlike his two earlier successful works which were both thrillers, this was a novel set in, "a small Scottish seaport town", and for Bo'nessians there was the added interest of trying to identify their friends and neighbours among the characters.

Reading Mr Sleath's new book would certainly have provided some light relief from the contents of the daily papers which were full of stories about the terrible troubles in Ireland, events in Russia and letters to the editor complaining about the new silver coins which were about to be introduced.

Somehow things don't seem to have changed all that much since Queen Elizabeth from Kinneil School was crowned sixty-two years ago, but let's hope at least the weather will be better when another Kinneil School lassie is next crowned Queen.

Set Fair with the Grangers

No man did more for Bo'ness Fair than Alex Ritchie. As teacher, headmaster, community councillor and latterly as secretary to Bo'ness Fair Festival Committee he worked tirelessly for the Fair.

This article was written on the eve of his retirement as headmaster of the Grange School and is reprinted as a tribute to a man whom I admired.

Mr. Ritchie's first connection with Fair came in 1912, when as a very small boy, only just begun school, he was chosen by the two Miss Dotts, Bo'ness Public School's famous and much beloved infant mistresses, to be one of their presentees. "I was clad from head to foot in a bright red suit, covered with little green leaves," recalls Mr. Ritchie. "For the Public School's presentees that year were the Babes in the Wood. The other poor lost Babe was Jennie Ainslie and together we wandered hand in hand through the streets of Bo'ness. The crowds seemed huge and I can still remember the cheers as we went up to bow to Queen Annie Peace from the Public School."

Next year Mr. Ritchie swopped his red suit as one of the Babes in the Wood for one of the red caps worn in those days by all Public School pupils, both boys and girls, when they went to the fair and together with his classmates from the second infant room watched the crowning of Alice McNaught from St. Mary's. But for him the highlight of the Fair was not the coronation ceremony, impressive though it no doubt was, but the thrill of being allowed to ride round the procession route on a hay cart and of looking down through the spaces in the slats at the big red wheels turning round and round. In 1914, when Academy Queen, Helen Grant, was crowned, he was not so lucky, because by then he had moved up from the infants and as a big boy in Primary One was considered old enough to walk round the whole route. "But in those days we thought nothing of walking despite the dust and the tar which always seemed to stick to the new white rubbers which were considered an essential part of our Fair outfits," adds Mr. Ritchie.

It was, however, to be quite a few weeks before the tar was to stick to Mr. Ritchie's shoes again, because less than three weeks after that warm July Fair Friday in 1914, Britain went to war with Germany. By 1919 when the return of peace made it possible for Joan Campbell from Borrowstoun School to be crowned as the first post-war Queen, Alex Ritchie was ready for the Academy, and when it came that school's turn to provide the main characters he was chosen as Lord in Waiting to Queen Catherine Sneddon. The Lord in Waiting's most important duty is to escort the presentees when they mount the platform to bow to the Queen and Mr. Ritchie remembers in particular accompanying Infant Mistress Grace Ross's choice of presentees. "Typical of her sense of humour, instead of the nursery rhyme characters such as Bo-Peep and Dick Whittington and his Cat, which were the usual presentees in those days, Miss Ross had cast two of her infants as Fish Supper and Vinegar. It was a dreadful job negotiating the steep stairs up to the throne with the wee boy who represented Vinegar, for he was dressed as a giant bottle with only tiny holes for his feet. My struggles to guide him up and down to the throne without 'a spill' obviously did not pass unnoticed, because the following Friday the *Journal* commented that, 'The young Lord in Waiting seemed inexperienced in handling a bottle'."

Mr. Ritchie remembers 1925, not only because of his role in the Fair, but also because it was in the October of that year he began his studies at Edinburgh University. By 1929 he had graduated, completed his teacher training at Moray House and returned to Bo'ness to join the staff of the Grange School in time to join in the preparations for the crowning of Grange School Queen, Marion Kilpatrick.

On that Fair day, fifty-three years ago, as the newest and youngest member of the Grange School's staff, Mr. Ritchie could hardly have foreseen the time when he would become headmaster of that same school. Now on the eve of his retirement Mr. Ritchie has given pride of place on the main stairway of the new extension to the Grange to a display of photographs of all the Fair Queens chosen from among its pupils.

"I can remember them all apart from Ina Ritchie, who was Queen in 1911," recalls Mr. Ritchie. "There's Annie Currie; she's Mrs. Serafini now. And Andrea Walker, the first Grange School Queen from the primary school after the closure of the secondary department following the opening of the new Academy. Then in 1946 it was the Grange School which had the honour to restart the Fair after the war, when Sadie Potter was crowned Queen."

All the colour photographs, of which Mr. Ritchie is so proud, have been presented to the Grange School by Mr. Archibald Buchanan, who was Queen Ina Ritchie's Champion away back in 1911. In addition, Mr. Buchanan has also arranged with Mr. Ritchie to have photographs taken of this year's Queen, and of all future Grange School Queens, so that the school at which he was once a pupil, will always have a complete record of its links with the Fair.

What makes Mr. Ritchie even more impressed by Mr. Buchanan's generous gift of the pictures and of a sum of money which has been invested to provide a gift for every future Grange School Queen, is the fact that Mr. Buchanan has for many years stayed south of the border in Skipton, Yorkshire. Despite his long exile, however, Mr. Buchanan has always remained in close touch with the Fair through the younger members of his family who still stay in Bo'ness, and it is this family interest in the Fair which Mr. Ritchie claims has always most impressed him with the Fair.

28

"Bo'ness Fair is not like other local gala days, which have customs grafted on to them simply to provide something to do. Bo'ness Fair is a tradition, a tradition which every Bo'ness child is brought up to respect, a fact which is clearly demonstrated by the amount of self discipline which the boys and girls show as they carry out their duties during the coronation ceremony," says Mr. Ritchie. "The Fair is also important for the way in which it brings exiled Bo'nessians back home, and for me no matter how famous the show business personalities appearing at the Royal Revels in the Douglas Park, the top of the bill attraction will always be simply the opportunity to wander round meeting old acquaintances whom I haven't seen for years."

One way in which Mr. Ritchie has managed to maintain family interest in the Fair as far as Grange School parents are concerned, has been to greatly increase the number of presentees so that as far as possible all Grange School pupils have the chance to be a character at the Fair at

The Deacon who led the march at the old style Bo'ness Miners Fair complete with sword and floral headress.

29

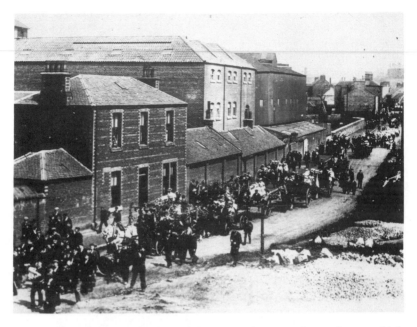

One of the original Fair processions. Note the many horse drawn vehicles a Bo'ness tradition which the town owed to the many carters who carried salt, coal and goods to and from the harbour and docks.

least once during their school careers. It was in fact Mr. Ritchie who introduced the new style presentees, now adopted by all the other schools, when he presented his all singing, all dancing Black and White Minstrels, which many people still recall with enthusiasm. So successful, indeed, were the young Minstrels that the group was kept together for several months and its appearances raised sums of money for various local charities.

Mr. Ritchie's other big contribution to the development of the Fair as a major spectacle was his decision to transform the exterior of his school on the Fair E'en into a floodlit fairy wonderland. This effort proved so successful that it, too, was taken up by other schools.

We end these reminiscences with those of the late ex-Bailie Mr. Robert Baptie, of Marchlands Avenue, for they very aptly sum up the feelings of all Bo'nessians, whether they were fortunate enough to be born in our old grey town by the Forth or have wisely made it their home by adoption as in his case.

Mr. Baptie writes "Though not a native of Bo'ness, I am a true Bo'nessian in my love of the Fair. As Convener of the Fair Committee I have visited Children's Days in many parts of the country, but no where have I seen anything to equal, far less surpass, our own Festival.

"Looking back over the years I see a long series of sunny days, for "bright Sol" seems to have favoured us. One disastrous morning, the rain poured down; all seemed set for an indoor coronation, but the Provost contacted the weather station at Pitreavie who said the rain would clear. The coronation was postponed for an hour — and the sun shone..

"Few people realise how much the success of the Fair depends on the devoted work of the school teachers. To mention names would be invidious, but we can all remember the stalwarts of the past, whose places are now being ably filled by the mini-skirted generation".

"To me, the most memorable Fair was that on the fiftieth anniversary. From far and near they came — the former Queens — from the Queen the previous year to the first Queen of all. This was indeed an indication of the cherished tradition of proud pageantry which has woven itself into the rich tapestry of the Bo'ness Children's Fair Festival."

Chapter 3

A Gala for Grangemouth

The success of Bo'ness Fair soon attracted attention in many neighbouring towns and just as Bo'ness had copied its celebrations from those of Lanimer Day in Lanark, so in turn its new style festivities were duly copied.

Amongst the first places to decide to stage its own Children's Day was that great Bo'ness rival, Grangemouth and there it was my grandfather William Hendrie who was the instigator. He was known throughout his long career in local government as "The Battling Bailie" and fortunately this was one of the many campaigns which he won and so on Friday 17th August 1906 the children of Grangemouth enjoyed their first gala day.

On that warm summer Friday over 2000 boys and girls formed up at Charing Cross and marched in a huge procession to Kerse House, the home of the Dundas family. It must have been a very colourful affair, because all of the children wore different coloured ribbons in their school colours. Those from Grange wore royal blue, while those from Dundas Primary wore scarlet, Zetland, yellow and Sacred Heart, green. The smallest children from the Infant School wore white, while, at the other end of the age range the senior boys and girls from Grangemouth High carried streamers in black and gold, the colours which they still proudly sport to this day.

Even more colour was added to Grangemouth's Children's Day as the gala has always been officially known, when in 1909 the crowning of a school girl queen was added to the festivities. This time Bailie Hendrie had the added satisfaction of seeing his youngest son, my father Nelson Patrick, play the part of one of the two page boys who in their white uniforms and cocked hats escorted Grangemouth's first Queen, High School pupil Nancy Baxter, who later became Mrs. Bruce Peddie.

From then on Mrs. Peddie always took a great interest in each successive Children's Day and on two occasions presented new fur trimmed robes for use on the big day. She was also honoured on two occasions by being invited to crown two of her young successors, Miss Mabel Malcolmson in 1933 and Miss Dorothy Gilmour, who was Grangemouth's Golden Jubilee Queen in 1959.

Like Mrs. Peddie, both of the queens whom she crowned were pupils of Grangemouth High School, but over the years all of the town's primary and secondary schools have taken it in turn to provide the town's reigning monarch. The Children's Day has been held faithfully every year with the exception of those during the First and Second World Wars and in addition to the schools already mentioned those supplying the royal court in-

Former Grangemouth Gala Queens gather for the town's Centenary Year Fair in 1972.

clude Beancross Primary, Bowhouse Primary and Grangemouth's unique Middle Schools, Moray and Abbotsgrange Road.

Ever since the second gala day, which was held on Saturday 24th June, 1907, Grangemouth has held its Children's Day on the Saturday nearest to this day in June. In addition to the procession and crowning ceremony

Grangemouth Gala Queen in 1953 May Ramsay from Grange School.

the festivities in the beautiful setting of the town's Zetland Park include sports and displays ranging from gymnastics and majorettes to radio controlled model ships sailing on the park's large boating pond.

Another link with Grangemouth's role as one of Scotland's most important ports has always been the abundance of flags and bunting available for the decoration of the town and decorated house frontages are now an especially spectacular feature of the festivities with Walt Disney cartoon characters and television favourites vying with the more traditional fairy tales and pantomimes as sources of inspiration.

At night Grangemouth's gala day is always rounded off with visits to the shows whose roundabouts and side stalls always occupy the same site on the banks of the Grange Burn. With this excellent large flat site, Grangemouth's shows have always far outrivalled those crowded into Corbiehall fairground at Bo'ness Fair and Grangemouth Children's Day has always enjoyed a special relationship with Scotland's show folks who always present a gift to the town's young queen.

Over sixty Grangemouth girls have now enjoyed that honour and in 1972 when Queen Fiona Fairlie from Bowhouse Primary was crowned

Typical of the many pictures taken at galas throughout the area in the 1940's and 1950's are these photos of youngsters watching the Grangemouth Children's Day procession. Notice the tables set for the street party tea after the procession passed by.

Queen many of her predecessors returned to mark the burgh's centenary year. Children's Day itself has now passed its 75th anniversary, and with all the obvious enthusiasm for it in Grangemouth it too looks set to go on to notch up its century, which would undoubtably have convinced my grandfather Hendrie that his fight to raise sufficient funds to launch the first gala in 1906 was well worth while.

Chapter 4

Linlithgow Marches

"Dreamthorp", that was what 19th century essayist Alexander Smith called Linlithgow. Whether or not Linlithgow was as sleepy a little town as he cared to paint it is a matter for conjecture, but one thing is certain that on one day each year it awoke from any "Brigadoon" like slumber and became the liveliest place in Scotland, when on the first Tuesday after the second Thursday in June, its inhabitants celebrated the age old ceremony of the Riding of the Marches.

To begin with, however, it was not always on the traditional "first Tuesday" that the magistrates and burgesses set out to inspect the boundaries of the lands, given to the town by King Robert II when he created Linlithgow a Royal Burgh in 1389.

At first the inspection of the "lands from Avon to the sea", which the King had given to the town, was very much a necessity, rather than a ceremony, for in those strife torn days, it was essential to make it absolutely clear to rivals that the people of Linlithgow intended to keep what belonged to them. During these early years, therefore, inspections probably took place as and when the magistrates learned of any damage to the march or boundary stones, but it may well have been a condition of the original charter that one formal visitation be made each year.

Little is known about these first inspections, except that they were made on foot and that this was almost certainly dictated by the fact that what roads there were in the area were in such a primitive state that they were little more than tracks.

It is generally accepted that the first actual riding of the marches took place in 1541, a year after the appointment of Linlithgow's first Provost, Henry Forrest. On 19th October 1541 the Burgh records contain the entry, "That all common lands of the Burghmuir and utherus and all common passages als weill and wyndes within the same be visitit seigne and considerit ieirlie upon Pasche Tuesday be the Provost, Baillies and consale and hale communitie and reformit and mendit quhaid need be."

Six months later on 17th April 1542 we read, "The Assays ordains the Provost, Bailies to set ane day that the consale and hale communitie mychtt pass about the common lands and to sett Marches as wis is of uther borrows." It is especially interesting to note that from the very outset the emphasis was on the "hale communitie" participating in the Marches as it has continued to do until this day.

At first both the weather and religion appear to have entered into the actual choice of date. The weather seems to have persuaded the Provost and Baillies to wait long enough for spring to promise a reasonable day and especially reasonable conditions under foot, but not too long so that any ravishes that the winter might have effected could be put right without too much delay. With this in mind, together with the fact that the inspection up until the Reformation, like English Rogation day ceremonies included the blessing of the boundary stones and the lands which they enclosed by a priest, appears to have influenced the choice of Pache Tuesday, the Tuesday before Easter as the date for the earliest Marches.

This of course meant that the first Marches fell during Lent and as this was a time for fasting this must have inhibited the feasting and drinking, which became such a feature in future years. Perhaps therefore this accounts for the subsequent change of date to the Tuesday after Whitsun.

Finally in 1767 the Provost, Magistrates and Councillors decided that the town's Whitsun Fair should be held on the second Thursday of June with the Riding of the Marches on the following Tuesday. Two hundred years ago diaries and calendars were far from common and so the inhabitants committed the Marches date to memory by reminding themselves that the big day would fall on the now famous "First Tuesday after the Second Thursday in June." Thus a tradition was born and with the exception of the years during the First and Second World Wars and the year of the General Strike in 1926 when celebrations were limited by law, it has continued to be observed in time honoured fashion ever since.

Having thus fixed a date, who then, in addition to the Provost and Magistrates rode these early Marches?

The answer is the members of Linlithgow's eight Societies of Incorporated Trades and the six Fraternities or Friendly Societies, each led by their respective Deacons.

Today the installation of the Deacons still makes a colourful Saturday evening preliminary to the Marches, but whereas now these officials are chosen specially for the big day, originally they were elected for a whole year and governed the affairs of their trades and fraternities through their special Deacon's Courts.

Linlithgow's eight Incorporated Trades in the earliest order in which they are recorded as Riding the Marches in 1687 were the Hammermen, the Tailors, the Baxters, the Cordiners, the Weavers, the Wrights, the Coopers and the Fleshers.

The Hammermen included all the smiths in the town from the blacksmiths and farriers right through to the silversmiths and jewellers. It is also possible that during the years when Linlithgow boasted Scotland's royal mint, which is believed to have stood near the site of the railway station that its workers would also belong to this guild.

The Tailors and Weavers are self explanatory. The Baxters were the bakers of whom a few remain in business in the town, including the famous Oliphants whose home made rolls, pies, tea breads, cakes and other delicacies far outrival anything which the giant multiples' recipes ever produce.

The Cordiners were Linlithgow's highly skilled shoemakers of whom the Morrisons are the last remaining family, although now only the retail and not the manufacturing side of their High Street business remains.

The Wrights, included all the town's joiners, carpenters, cabinet makers and coach builders.

The Coopers covered all of the barrel makers at the town's breweries and at St Magdalene Distillery and may possibly have taken in other workers from these establishments.

Finally the Fleshers were the butchers and slaughter house employees. They were undoubtedly one of the oldest groups in the town, but do not appear to have been recognised as a fully fledged Incorporated Guild until the middle of the 16th century when they replaced the Guild of Walkers, which was the accepted name for the Cloth Fullers, and took their place in the Marches procession.

It is interesting to find that each Trade Guild had its own particular meeting place in one of Linlithgow's many inns or taverns.

For their headquarters the Fleshers had the oldest inn in the town, the Black Bitch at West Port, which while it took its name from Linlithgow's legendary greyhound, recognised its close connection with the butchers

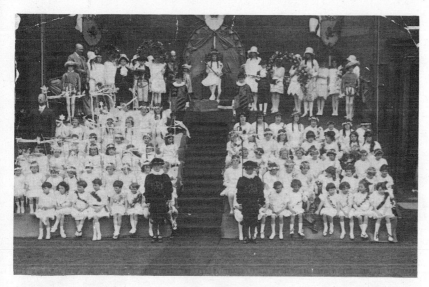

The crowning of little Queen Elizabeth Kay from Kinneil Primary School in 1928.

The scene at the coronation of Queen Margaret Henderson in 1951. Provost Hanney is seen behind the microphone but apart from the people very little has changed from the picture above.

41

Queen Elizabeth with her pages Billy Sneddon and John Taylor in 1962.

The gathering of former Queens who attended the Bo'ness Tercentenary Fair in 1968. The Tercentenary celebrations recalled the fact that permission to hold the very first Bo'ness Fair was granted to the Duchess Anna of Kinneil by Charles II in 1668. These first fairs were of course farming rather that festive occasions.

Queen Margaret Carson and her pages from Bo'ness Academy in 1949 This picture shows Queen Margaret attending the Royal Revels which that year were held in the Academy Playing Field, Grahamsdyke Road.

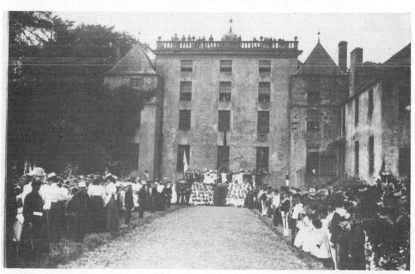

One of the earliest pictures of a Bo'ness Fair Coronation which was held on this occasion in front of Kinneil House, complete with its towers, which are now being restored, cupola and balustrade.

An early Fair arch erected at the miners' rows at the Snab. Note the beautifully clipped box wood and the Bo'ness coat of arms of a sailing ship and motto "Sine Metu", "Without Fear".

This very spectacular arch was erected outside the old distillery with Fison's Chemical Works in the background.

44

Lady in Waiting Jean Forbes (now Mrs. G. C. Fettis) photographed in front of one of the small decorative arches which are such a feature of Bo'ness Fair festivities.

A Venetian Fantasy. One of Bobby Heath's many prize winning designs.

Doris-Anne Aitken (now Mrs. P. Aitken) as Queen of the Fairies.

Presentees Toothpaste and Toothbrush (Douglas Snedden) in a pre war Fair procession.

45

Butcher Sandy Rankine's pony and trap.

Willie "Topping" Neilson poses proudly with Darkie pulling the famous "Little Bo Peep" float with its live sheep. Darkie, who, shows clearly the origin of the old Bo'ness saying "All dressed up like a Fair horse", was always regarded at the Co-op as "belonging" to Willie's brother Davie who was the foreman at the transport department. He always took Darkie out on the baker's round and earned his nickname "Doughnuts" from his fondnest for the product which he sold.

46

Another view of the "shows" in Corbiehall. Notice the tall masted sailing ship in the harbour in the background of the picture.

All the fun of the "shows" in their traditional setting of Corbiehall. Notice the procession winding its way past the booths and roundabouts and in particular the pupils, both boys and girls wearing their school caps.

Bo'ness and Carriden Band traditionally lead Grange School in the procession. This picture shows band members of a former year.

Bathgate Caledonian Pipe Band photographed around 1904.

48

through its very unusual sign. This took the shape of a butcher's copy of a plaque and depicted the tools of the flesher's trade, the knife and cleaver. An actual stone butcher's plaque also sat on the pub counter, but unfortunately this ancient relic was lost after a fire during the 1930's. Members of the Ingram family, who owned the Black Bitch at the time of the blaze recall the slab being carried with debris out of the bar and into the backyard. It was never seen again and may well have been carted away with the rubbish. Fortunately the date carved on the stone plaque was recorded and as this date 1284 was also recorded on the inn sign it would appear likely that it was either the date of the opening of the Black Bitch or the year of the Incorporation of the Guild of Fleshers.

Further along the High Street another inn, which still remains to this day, the well known Swan, recently renamed The Armoury, was always known as the home of the Guild of Wrights. It did not always enjoy the best of reputations in earlier times as it was also patronised by Linlithgow's nail makers, who were always considered as rather disreputable as they were originally "tinker tykes".,The reason many of the nailers frequented the Swan was that one of their crowded little workshops was situated right behind it and this small ivy covered detached outhouse can still be seen behind the inn, standing in one of Linlithgow's now unique long narrow run rig type gardens which ran from behind the High Street buildings right down to the loch.

All the nails produced in Linlithgow were hand made and this appears to have been drouthy work for it was often alleged that the nail makers spent more time in the Swan than they did in their crowded work shop. Perhaps the nailers may have used the excuse that this was good for orders, for the Swan as well as being the haunt of the members of the Guild of Wrights was also the drinking place of the snabs or cobblers, whose official headquarters of their Guild of Cordiners was right next door at Cordiners or Cordiners' land.

Further along the High Street at Number 123 can still be seen the badge of the Incorporated Guild of Cordiners while above the door of the next door house, Number 125, where the 1871 census records 4 shoemakers and one leather worker as having their home, there appears a carving of the Guilds emblem of an oak leaf. The connection between the leather trade and the oak leaf was that its bark was put in the water in which the hides were steeped in order to supply the all important tanning.

Another of the incorporated Guilds, the Hammermen, had their base in another of the town's inns, which is still in business, the Red Lion, but sometime down through the ages it has undergone a change of colour for it was originally always referred to as the Golden Lion. The Lion was originally built as a private house by the Kae family in 1625. They were well known as the town's surgeons, but as a side line they were also what were known as King's Sergeants, which gave them the right to collect local taxes and it was when local folk came to pay their dues that the Lion first became a drinking howf.

Latterly the Red Lion as it had by then become, became the meeting place for the Deacon and his followers from Nobels Explosives Factory, when it opened on 16th September 1902 and they continued to gather there when the factory was taken over by I.C.I.

Another of the more modern groups, the Paper Makers, chose the Jubilee Arms as the headquarters for their Deacon. The Jubilee, which was originally owned by the Learmouth family, stood where the High Street flats now rise and after it was taken over by Mrs Brock its name was changed to the Windsor Buffet. It was particularly well known for its outdoor quoiting pitches.

To return to the original eight incorporated craft guilds, each used its respective inn as the setting for its court, which was presided over by its Deacon assisted and advised by My Lord, who had been Deacon the year before and by their Left Hand Man who had himself been Deacon, two years previously. Using their combined experience they met regularly to fix the prices for their Guild's products and acted to ensure that they were never undercut by rivals from other towns, who might try to set up stalls at Linlithgow's weekly markets. They also decided who were to be admitted to their Guild and in particular who were to be allowed to begin apprenticeships. Then once boys had signed articles and become apprentices the Deacon and his two henchmen were particularly responsible for them. First they had to ensure that the Master provided the boy with clothes, food and shelter and then that the apprentice in his turn gave good service. Finally the Deacon and his court were charged with setting the examinations which at the end of five or seven years decided whether the apprentice should be recognised as a time served journeyman.

In addition to holding their own regular courts, the Deacons of the Incorporated Trades, who would incidentally be re-elected for several years, were also important in the burgh as they were always elected Town

Councillors, subject to their approval by the Provost, the four Magistrates or Baillies and the other Councillors who were mainly merchants.

Unlike the Deacons of the eight incorporated trades, the Deacons of the Fraternities did not have a place amongst the 27 strong Town Council, but their friendly societies did have an important part to play in the life of the town in these days, long before the coming into being of the "welfare state".

The six Fraternities were, the Gardeners, the Tanners, the Whipmen, the Skinners, the Curriers and the Dyers, of whom only the last still takes an active part in the Marches.

Unlike the Trade Guilds, people did not have to be members of a craft to belong to a Fraternity and indeed today there is not one dyer in the Dyers.

The role of the Fraternities was to provide welfare benefits such as sickness pay, widows pensions and even burial payments for members and their families. Like the Trade Guilds the Fraternities had their own meeting places in the town's taverns, of which Linlithgow had apparently no shortage as the Free Church minister writing in 1876 noted that the burgh had no fewer than 37 licensed premises to serve its 3,600 of a population.

For the Dyers the meeting place has been St Michael's Hotel since it was built in typically Victorian style in the High Street in 1886 and it is there that they still hold their Marches breakfast. The Dyers are the last remaining Fraternity in the town to take an active part in the Marches celebrations and they are also reckoned to be one of the oldest. The earliest document in their possession is dated 3rd January 1670 and states that, "George Dicksone, lidster, burges of Linlithgow receaved from Thomas Heart laitt Baillie of the Burgh of Linlithgow, present Deacons of the Incorporation of Dyers of said Burge, in the name of bretherine of the incorporation, the soume of Ane Hundredd Marks Scots Money."

Originally the Dyers were Lidsters of cloth, cloth walkers and cloth fullers and while all of these occupations have long since ceased ro exist in the town, Lidster like Baxter does survive as a well known local name.

Even as early as the beginning of the 18th century, however when there were plenty of actual dyers in the town, the Fraternity appears to have been willing to consider admitting other townfolks to its ranks for at is recorded that on 4th April 1728, "David Sands, Merchant, R Forrester,

Writer, and Alex. Duncan, Wright were admitted."

The Dyers do however appear to have been particular about whom they admitted because it is noted in their minute book that, "admission was refused to a member of the Incorporation of Smiths", despite his plea "to be the son-in-law of a dyer."

Throughout the 18th century the Dyers did a great deal of charitable work. For instance on 5th June 1736 it is noted that "12/- were given by order of several members to a poor stranger," thus living up to Linlithgow's proud motto that "St Michael is kind to strangers." On the same day 6 pence was given to "a poor girl whose leg was cut off." Sickness benefit and pensions were provided and dirge money was frequently provided to ensure that members had a funeral of which they could be proud. One such entry reads, "To spent at Brother Smith's dirge £1 10s. 0d."

By the beginning of the 19th century the Fraternity had officially incorporated itself as a Society of Relief and throughout Victorian times did much charitable work. It also aided and supported the Town Council. For instance in 1832 the Dyers contributed £20 to help with the repairs to the Town House on condition that they could hold their meetings there. This was agreed and a further £20 was donated in 1848 towards the upkeep of the Italian style Town House with its covered pizza, where the double staircase now exists.

Today as already mentioned there are no longer any dyers in the Dyers, but their members proudly carry on their Fraternity's customs and ensure that their banner, gifted by former Deacon Thomas Mickle when he was their oldest member, is still held high in the Marches procession, just as their Deacon still holds equal pride in wearing their beautiful gold chain of office.

As the traditional Trade Guilds and Fraternities have disappeared it is fortunate that other groups of workers and their social groups within the town such as the paper workers and the Forty One Club have come forward to take their places so that on at least two Saturday evenings prior to the big day, the town's hostelries are alive and the High Street crowded as these bodies combine with the Dyers to keep alive the custom of chairing the Deacons.

All along the High Street as far as the Low Port the Deacons are borne before their supporters carry them the traditional three times around the Cross. During recent years each newly installed Deacon and My Lord

52

have then been received on the steps of the Town House by the Provost who invites them to partake of the Loving Cup. Amongst scenes of great excitement and cheering from the large crowds which always gather, the Deacon is then chaired once more and led by a local band returns with his followers to their headquarters in one of the High Street inns to get into the Marches spirit.

After the lively installations of the Deacons on the Saturday evenings before the Marches, the next traditional ceremony in preparation for the day itself is the Crying, which always takes place at one o'clock on the preceding Friday.

As townfolk could be fined if they did not take part in the Riding of the Marches, it was obviously very important that everyone in the burgh should be reminded of the forthcoming event and so at lunchtime on the Friday, Linlithgow's Town Crier makes his way along the full length of the High Street from Low Port to West Port and at set intervals, introduced by "tuck of drum", announces, "O Yez, O Yez, O Yez. The burgesses, craftsmen and whole inhabitants of the Royal Burgh of Linlithgow are hearby warned and summoned to attend my Lord Provost, Baillies and Council at the ringing of the bells on Tuesday 20th June curt, for the purpose of riding the Town's Marches and liberties according to the use and custom of the ancient and honourable Burgh and that in their best carriage, equipage, apparel and array and also to attend all diets of court held and appointed on that day by my Lord Provost and Baillies and that under the penalty of One Hundred Pounds Scotch each. God save the Queen and my Lord Provost."

As well as the drummer the Town Crier is always accompanied by two uniformed halbediers and equally traditionally by the town's school bairns, who follow the little entourage from the first stop at Lowport where the Whitten Fountain once stood and where a more prosaic keep left sign now fills its place right along the flag bedecked High Street past freshly painted shop fronts and traditionally newly white washed closes to the final crying at West Port, where the 700 pupils of Linlithgow Primary swell the crowd.

One bairn who clearly recalled these annual Friday escapes from the routine of the classroom was David Morrison, a Black Bitch exiled in New York, who wrote home from the States as follows, "I see myself again as a Burgh School pupil, longing for the Friday preceding the great event, when the town herald Jock the Blackie, attired in his new velvet suit

53

with red stockings and buckled shoes and cocked bonnet and feather, gathered us all around him for the Crying. Like a great orchestra leader he would direct and time us with his drum stick in the opening "O Yez, O Yez, O Yez" of his proclamation. Again I am keeping step to "roke", played by flautist Muir and drummer Bowie as I find myself marching along the High Street with my school mates. I leave the crowd at the Cross and return to the Burgh School, realising that if I were late "Baldie" or "Bull Dog" Walker or "Coal Jock" Forrester would greet me with the tawse."

With Linlithgow's great leather making tradition its interesting to wonder if the tawse was made right here in Linlithgow by old Gillespie the sadler.

Today the town's children still faithfully follow the Crying, but now they have no need to fear the strap on their return to the classroom, for lunchtime is officially extended and as far as the boys and girls of Linlithgow Primary are concerned the entourage is in fact welcomed into their playground at West Port where the final reading of the proclamation is made. Then their duty done the Town Crier and his retinue go off to slake their thirsts with the youngsters' familiar chant of "O Yez, O Yez, O Yez, half a pound of the store's rotten cheese," still echoing in their ears.

"There was an auld wife had a wee pickle tow, And she wad gae try the spinning o' t."

It's to these words and the tune that goes with them, Linlithgow's own tune, "The Roke and the Wee Pickle Tow", that Dreamthorp awakes on Marches Morn.

5 a.m. may seem early, far too early for any other morning of the year, but it can never be too early on Marches Morn as the flautists parade the High Street to waken the lieges. Originally according to the town's well known local historian Mr George Arthur, the early start to Marches Morn was very necessary as all of the burgh's financial accounts had to be balanced and laid before the Provost at his breakfast to prove that all was well before the Riding could begin. Today the most devoted of the Marches enthusiasts are equally anxious that everything should be just right for Linlithgow's biggest day of the year and they think nothing of staying up all night to put the final finishing touches to the weeks of work, which have gone into the production of their special decorated floats, details of which are kept a closely guarded secret until they emerge in all their glory for the judging on Marches Morn.

Three hours have still to go before the floats and huge tableaux trundle along the High Street to the Vennel Car Park, when at 6 a.m. the flautists are joined in their preambulation of the burgh by a piper and drummer, who are joined by a considerable crowd as they halt to play and receive suitable refreshments at the homes of the Provost, Chairman of the Community Council and other well known townsfolk.

By now the whole town is well and truly awake and stirring, ready to welcome the arrival of the first band shortly after 7 a.m. Most often this honour seems to have fallen to Kinneil Silver Band, whose playing of "Hail Smiling Morn" as they march down St Ninian's Road towards West Port, means the Marches to so many Black Bitches. For on this special day of the year all the old rivalries between Linlithgow and Bo'ness, or Borrowstounness to give the old port its full title, are forgotten and the Garvies from over Flints even forgive the Black Bitches for the time when the Provost and Magistrates of the Royal and Ancient Burgh ordered gibbets to be erected at the West Port and the Low Port on which to hang any Bo'nessian who dared try enter.

In a way however it is on Marches Morn that rivalries between the two neighbouring towns should be at their highest, because it is on this day that Linlithgow remembers its links with its out port Blackness, which was once Scotland's second most important harbour and it was the challenge of the new harbour at Bo'ness, the Burgh Town on the Point three miles further up the Forth in the 17th century that originally provoked all the competition, still existing in somewhat friendlier fashion to this day. On Marches day, however Bo'nessians have a special reason for burying ancient hatchets and wishing Linlithgow well, because it is a well known belief that whatever weather the Marches gets Bo'ness Fair always gets the same.

Come sun or rain however the Marches still go on and following Kinneil Band come three or four others each Marches Morn, including these Bo'ness stalwarts Carriden, with whom Kinneil have as much if not more rivalry than exists between the two burghs. Over the years other bands which have played at the Marches include Bathgate Caledonian Pipe Band, Broxburn Silver Band, Dr Guthrie's Boy's Pipe Band, Philipstoun Pipe Band, Armadale Silver Band Winchburgh Brass Band, Camelon Brass Band, Falkirk and District United Trades Band, Wallacetone and District Pipe Band, Avon Valley Pipe Band, Whitburn Miners' Welfare Silver Band and of course the town's own bands,

Linlthgow and District Pipe Band and Linlithgow's famous Reed Band.

Last year the bands were even joined by one from Germany, but now matter where the bands come from they are all expected to master Linlithgow's own tune, "The Roke and Wee Pickle Tow" sometimes known by the more dignified title of "Lord Lithgow's March".

"The Roke" is however essentially a weaving tune and with Linlithgow's long connection with the textile trade it is possible that this is how the tune became so closely associated with the town. Originally however it appears to have been writen by an Aberdeenshire schoolmaster, Alexander Ross, who was dominie of the little village school at Kincardine O'Neil for 36 years during the 18th century. Ross was born in Torphins in 1699 and died at Lochee in Forfarshire in 1784. He published the "Roke" in 1768 in a song book called "Helenore or the Fortunate Shepherdess", which was printed in Aberdeen. It must have proved popular for eight years later in 1776 it was republished in "Herd's Collecton".

Originally "The Roke" was much longer than it is today, with no fewer than 19 verses each of 8 lines, but subsequent books abreviated it to the first and final three verses as is played and sung today.

"THE ROKE AND THE WEE PICKLE TOW"

There was an auld wife had a wee pickle tow
And she wad gae try the spinnin o't,
But lootin her down, her rock took a low
And that was a bad beginnin' o't.
She sat and she grat, and she flat, and she flang,
And she threw and she blew, and she wriggled and wrang,
And she chokit and bakit, and cried like to mang,
Alas for the dreary beginnin' o't.

I've wanted a sark for these auchty years and ten,
And this was to be the beginnin' o't,
But I vow I shall want it for as long again,
Or ever I try the spinnin' o't,
For never since ever the ca'd as they ca'me
Did sic a mishap and mischanter befa' me,
But she shall ha'e leave baith to hand and to draw me
The neist time I try the spinnin' o't.

57

I ha'e keepit my hoose now these three score o'years
And aye kept frae the spinnin' o't,
But how I was sarkit, foul fa' them that speirs
For it minds me o' the beginnin' o't.
But oor women are now-a-days a' grown sae brae
That ilka ane maun ha'e a sark, and some ha'e two—
The warld was better when ne'er ane ava,
Had a rag but ane at the beginnin' o't.

In the days they ca' yor gin auld folks could but get
To a surcoat, hough-syde, for the winnin' o't,
Of coat-raips weel cut by the cast o' their shape,
They never socht mair o' the spinnin' o't,
A pair o' grey toggers weel clinkit benew,
Of nae other lit but the hue of the ewe,
With a pair of rough mullions to scruff through the dew;
Was the fee they socht at the beginnin' o't.

But we maun ha'e linen, and that maun ha'e we,
And how get ye that but by spinnin' o't,
How can we ha'e face for to seek a great fee,
Except that we can help at the winnin' o't.
And we ha'e pearlies and marbles, and locks,
And some other things the ladies ca' smocks,
And how get we that gin we tak nee o'er rocks,
And pu' what we can at the spinnin' o't.

'Tis needless for us to mak' our remarks,
Fae our mithers miss-cookin' the spinnin' o't,
She never kenn'd ocht, o' the guid o' the sarks
Frae this a-back tae the beginnin' o't.
Twa three 'ell o' plqidin' was a' that bude be bocht,
For in ilka town sic an things was no' wrocht,
Sae little they kenn'd o' tha spinnin' o't.

Roke or Rock means the wooden distaff used in spinning. Pickle
means a small quantity. Tow is hemp in an unprepared state. Lout means
to bend and low is a flame.

According to Stenhouse in his notes to Johnston's Musical Museum, "The Roke" existed in an earlier state, whose "rather crude words" were cleaned up by Ross and this may well be true as the tune appears to have been known as early as 1724 when it is mentioned in "Ramsay's Tea Table Miscellany".

Versions of "The Roke" are said to exist as far away as Burgandy in France, but no matter what its origins it is very definitely Linlithgow's and its familiar jaunty tune is heard over and over again throughout the town as Marches Morn moves on towards 9 a.m. and the start of the equally traditional breakfasts.

The Provost's breakfast begins with the Town Crier, immaculate in uniform, calling the assembled guests from the Upper Hall of the Burgh Halls to the Lower Hall, where the long white clothed tables laden with fresh baked wheaten rolls, bran scones, flouries, honey and marmalade await them while the tempting smell of frying eggs and sizzling bacon waft from the kitchen. Nowadays gapefruit is the first course, whereas in the past the menu started with porridge followed by "saut herring", presumably to promote a drouth for the rest of the day's proceedings.

Not only menus have changed over the years, but also the venues for the breakfasts themselves, the Provost's breakfast being held for many years in The Star and Garter, while the Dyers sat down to dine at Upper Bonnytoun Farm. The farm was the setting for the Dyers' meal until the mid 1920's when they moved to St Micheal's Hotel where they dine to this day.

Even at such an early hour of the morning both of Linlithgow's Marches Breakfasts are famed for the wit and eloquence of their speakers, who always set the standard for the remainder of the day's many toasts and replies.

Speakers and guests at the Breakfasts often include many exiled Black Bitches returned specially for the big day from places as far apart as America and Australia, New Zealand and Nigeria, South Africa and even Saudi Arabia and thoughts always turn to those still abroad but who would equally dearly love to be back home for The Marches. Often their greetings are read out after the Breakfasts and their words form one of the most sentimental moments of the whole Marches Morn.

Once the speeches and greetings are over and definitely never later than 10.15, the Provost in his magnificent ermine trimmed robe and wearing the burgh's gleaming gold chain of office leads the Magistrates,

Councillors and guests from the Burgh Halls, up the steep Kirkgate, through the New Entry and into the Palace forecourt for the Kirkin'.

Soon after the Dyers in their black silk hats and in more recent years the members of the Forty One Club in their equally distinctive tweeds and deerstalkers also make their way in procession up the Kirkgate to St Michael's with its golden crown of thorns and there in the shadow of the ruins of the royal palace where Mary Queen of Scots was born in 1542, while the Deacons greet My Lord Provost, their followers fraternise, shake hands and bid each other "Happy Marches".

After the age old custom of Fraternising at The Palace, all concerned walked back down through the crowds who line the Kirkgate to the east side of the Cross, where the equally traditional ceremony of Fencing the Court takes place with the Town Clerk reading and the Town Crier announcing the following proclamation.

"I defend and I forbid in our Sovereign Lady's name, and in name of My Lord Provost, and Baillies of the Royal Burgh of Linlithgow, that no person or persons presume nor take upon hand, under whatever colour or pretext, to trouble or molest the Magistrates and Burgesses in their peaceful riding of the town's Marches under all highest pains and charges that after may follow. God save the Queen."

And so the actual Riding begins with the marshalling of the procession. One of the earliest mentions of the marshalling, which is a considerable and formidable task as it involves dozens of carriages and hundreds of eager participants, occurs in 1531, when the Weavers were ordered, "to pass ail together under their Deacon with their banners in their old use and wont of long time past the memory of man, betwixt the Baxters and the Tailors."

One of the best known Marshalls of the Marches procession was Henry Robinson who carried out this duty for many years at the turn of the century in his capacity of Superintendant of Police. Following old tradition he always began by ordering the Deacons to "walk forward and show themselves." When he was satisfied that all was in order he gave the signal for the whole procession to move off westwards along the crowd-packed narrow High Street, down the slope past the Spanish Ambassador's House and on through the cheers and shouts of "Happy Marches" to Linlithgow Bridge.

In the year 1900 the order of procession was
1   Bo'ness and Carriden Band

2 Carriage and four horses with My Lord Provost and the Magistrates,
3 Carriage and two horses with the Treasurer, Dean of Guild, Town Clerk and Fiscal,
4 Carriages with Councillors and Provost's Guests,
5 Incorporation of Hammermen,
6 Incorpration of Baxters,
7 Broxburn Silver Band,
8 Incorporation of Cordiners and Linlithgow Natives Association,
9 Incorporation of Wrights,
10 Masons
11 Fraternity of Tanners,
12 Fraternity of Whipmen (Carters),
13 Fraternity of Curriers,
14 Painters,
15 Pipe Band,
16 Distillery Employees,
17 Candlemakers,
18 Lochmill Paperworkers,
19 Good Templars,
20 Cricketers,
21 Football Clubs,
22 Other Societies in order as fixed with the Marshall,
23 Kinneil Band,
24 Fraternity of Dyers,
25 Private Carriages.

These private carriages like those of the Provost, Magistrates, Councillors and Guests were of course all horse drawn and the beautifully groomed horses and gleaming landaux of St Cuthbert's Co-operative Association in Edinburgh continued to carry the Provost and leading guests, but sadly they are the last remaining horses in the procession with all of the other participants in cars or floats. Today most of the decorated floats are pulled by tractors and gone forever are the magnificent stately Clydesdales with their plated manes and tails and their burnished horse brasses glittering in the Marches sun.

Another splash of colour missing from modern processions are all the banners and flags, which each Guild and Fraternity proudly bore in front of their ranks. As well as their own distinctive flag each guild also took great delight in making each float reflect its craft by including upon it the tools of its trade and examples of the wares which its members produced throughout the year. For instance the Hammermen's decorated cart bore a large hammer and anvil, while the Wright's pony trap which was decorated all over with curly wood shavings carried a small bench at which worked the cut out figures of two joiners whose arms sawed away, powered by elastic bands, pulled in turn by the youngest apprentice.

It was also the youngest apprentice's job to help gather the shavings needed to decorate the float. This job began many weeks before the Marches and went on nightly in the lofts of Brocks and Ritchies joiner shops. Traditionally the shavings were of yellow pine boards, as this wood was particularly suitable for the purpose as it was almost knot free. Long shavings were gathered to loop from one end of the cart to the other, while short light curly shavings were used as tassles to hang between the loops. During the 1930's attempts were made to produce technicolour shavings by dying the wood before running the shavings from it, but this was never very successful as only the side of the shavings could be treated.

Slogans were also very popular on the craft guild floats, the Cordiners boasting, "Our trade is ever lasting" and "True to the Last", while one baker asked, "Can man live by bread alone? Yes if it's Watson's."

As the procession makes its way westwards all of the town's many bells ring out, including those in the tower of the Burgh Halls as well as St Michael, Blessed St Mary and wee Meg Duncan in St Michael's and all the other church bells. Describing this mass bell ringing in his account of the "Church Bells of Linlithgowshire" written in 1912, F.C.Eeles wrote, "The bells cease as the procession passes out of sight over the Horse Market Head at the west end of the town. It then proceeds to Linlithgow Bridge."

While the crowds along the High Street and particularly those at the West Port are always enthusiastic, the villagers at the Brig are never out-done in the reception which they give the procession. At the old white washed inn the Waddie Loving Cup, donated by Alexander Spence the Deacon of the Dyers in 1922, is waiting filled to the brim to provide welcome refreshment, while at the same time refreshing the memories of all those who drink from it that the bridge over the River Avon marks the Western extremities of Linlithgow's boundaries.

How much more civilised is this pleasant method of aiding the memory on the subject of the town's bounds than the much commoner, but much

62

more painful one, found in many English towns of whipping the local school children at each march stone to beat into their memories what belonged to their burghs.

Half an hour later after various toasts, including one to the "Marches" and another to "The People of the Brig", which are drunk from the Loving Cup, the procession moves off again, eastwards this time back towards Linlithgow and as soon as it reappears past the Horse Market Head its return is spotted by the lookout at the top of the Town House clock tower who gives the signal for the bells to peal out anew to announce its safe return. The bells then continue above the cheers of the populace, according to Eeles, "while the procession passes eastwards on the way to Blackness. As it passes out of sight at the Duke's Entry, the ringing ceases."

Many of the larger floats now drop out of the procession at Low Port from which traditionally the race to Blackness began.

It was always considered to be a great honour to be the first carriage into the Square at Blackness, but on the last lap many carriages have traditionally made an unscheduled halt at the top of the brae leading down into the old sea port, at what is reliably reported to be the fastest growing hedge in the area, because of the annual watering, which it receives.

At Blackness all the participants are welcomed by the Baron Bailie. The post of Baron Bailie is unique to the village and dates back to medieval times, when the magistrates of Linlithgow felt that the three miles, which separated the town from its port made it impossible for them to ensure law and order around the harbour which was the second busiest in the whole of Scotland. They therefore decided to appoint a prominent villager to act in their name, a custom still faithfully maintained. The present Baron Bailie is village post master Robert Fleming and although unlike his predecessors he can no longer fine smugglers or flog wrongdoers, he still takes a lively interest in village happenings and each Marches Day delivers his annual report. Toasts are then drunk in Blackness milk, liberally laced with whisky, to give all present renewed energy to climb Castle Hill for the fencing of the court on the site of St. Ninians's Chapel. After a leisurely lunch all the participants return to Lowport ready for the climax of the whole day, when at 5 o'clock the bells ring out again and the procession rides along the High Street and thrice round the Cross Well. The foundation stone of the present well was laid on 4th June 1807 to mark the 69th birthday of King George III.

An inscription on the west side of the well records this occasion and also notes that it was "executed by Robert Gray, stone mason, Edinburgh." It is interesting to note that Gray had lost a hand and had had a small mallet fixed to the stump of his arm. His handicap does not seem to have hindered his work in any way and the well which cost £500, £400 of which had to be borrowed, is as fine an example of its kind as any in Scotland. It is hexagonal in form and has three basins and three platforms all of which are adorned with grotesque gargoyles and statues. A peaceful looking St Michael supports the town arms on the front, or south side, while on the east the town drummer and fifer herald the rising sun. To the West side is depicted the Town Officer wearing a scarf bearing the words "God Save the King". He is accompanied by another figure, sometimes said to be modelled on a Deacon of the period. Another figure appears on the north side of the well but who he represents is not recorded. Topping off all the statues and gargoyles is a unicorn, Scotland's original royal beast, from which the water is fed into three basins through the gargoyle faces.

Three is also the number of times that the procession circles the well and makes its way round the Cross and this tradition is again said to be a direct link with pagan times when three was considered to be a lucky number. Traditionally each time the procession circled the cross it did so at a faster pace until on the third run the coachmen whipped their tired horses to a gallop, but this dangerous practice has now stopped and the hugh crowd which is often the largest of the whole day is satisfied with the spectacle of the occasion without the risks which used to attend it.

When the procession has completed its third round and My Lord Provost and the Deacons have drunk each others healths on the steps of the Town House and bid each other "Safe oot, safe in", it is time for everyone present to unite in the singing of "Auld Lang Syne".

In the past it was then the custom of the Lord Provost to lead the Magistrates and Councillors down to Jimmy Tamson's Inn on the west side of the Vennel for dinner, while the crowd patronised other howfs including those already mentioned as headquarters for the Guilds and Fraternities and also the Crown and Anchor where the sea captains of Blackness used to congregate in Low Port, the Custom House in Bo'ness Road, the Crown opposite the Custom House, the Wheatsheaf in High Street opposite the Bo'ness Road turn, the Commercial on the corner of Preston Road or as it was formerly called Kipps Road and of course the Star and Garter which was known in the 18th century as Whitten's Inn because of its proprietor and outside of which the famous Whitten fountain used to stand.

For as long as can be remembered Marches Day has traditionally ended for the younger generation and those who are still young at heart with visits to "the shows". These roundabouts and booths have over the years occupied a variety of sites including Porteous Park, Learmonth's Park, the Park at the east side of the High Street, Stockbridge, Manse Park, Signal Box Field, Lochmill Siding, St John's Avenue and the area around where Katie Wearie's Tree stood until so very recently, but at no time were they more colourful than when they stretched from the Cross right along the loanings in the High Street.

Then they included hobby horses and sway boats, coconut shies and stookie dolls while hot ginger bread men were the culinary treat instead of the candy floss and ice cream of more modern times.

The first cinema shows ever given in Linlithgow came with the early Marches fairs, when Biddell's set up their tented moving picture show on the drying green at the West Port. Much earlier the Marches night crowds were entertained by a live drama about the Marches itself Entitled "Marches Day" It was written by a local shop keeper William Finlayson and is noted as having been reprinted in 1814 and is said to have lampooned the events of typical Riding.

Fun and celebrations go on late on Marches Night and next morning the townsfolk enjoy the luxury of a very long lie for the Wednesday is always regarded as "Recovery Day". Even after the townsfolk are up and about the town is deserted for it is as old a tradition as "Recovery Day" itself that it is the day of the summer for "Black Bitches" to go on trips and outings to places near and far. Before setting out however the bairns of the town have always traditionally made a special pilgrimage back to the field where the shows have now packed up and left town, for with any luck there is extra pocket money to be had for the picking up under the roll a penny stalls, the jungle ride and the chair o' planes.

Another attraction of former Recovery Days for the youngsters of the town was the sports which was held for a number of years at the East Bay at Blackness, but now the children have to wait for Gala Day on the first Saturday in June for anything to be officially organised for them.

Any suggestion however that Recovery Day has had its day and ought to be replaced by a Monday holiday before the Marches was however totally rejected when the local school council polled parents on the subject. It is good to know that even the new comers respect the town's old traditions.

Chapter 5

Linlithgow Yesterdays

One of the most fascinating glimpses of the history of past Marches is contained in the old programmes, which faithfully record not only the details of each big day, but the advertisements of the town's leading traders of the period.

In 1900 for instance Robert Jamieson, Grocer and Wine Merchants confidently recommended their "very fine blend of whisky at 2/6 a bottle for use as a beverage, a stimulant or for medical purposes." A bottle of "The Antiquary" cost the princely sum of 3/6 while a bottle of "Palace Liquer" cost all of 3/- as did "Brig O' Turk".

For the teetotal, Jamiesons offered tea at 1/8 per lb. and boasted, "no better to be had anywhere at the same price."

J. Hutton, Provision and Spirit Merchant also advertised tea at 1/6 per lb. with finest blend of Indian and Ceylon at 2/2, while George C. McNair at 73 High Street boasted of his own imports and blends of both tea and whisky. James T. Drinnan's offered whisky by the gallon while Richard Philip, 167 High Street, had Glenlivet at only 1/10. Still on the subject of whisky, licensed premises which advertised in the 1900 Marches programme included David Barclay's "The Auld Hole In the Wa' ", Joseph Braithwaite's "Cross Tavern" or "Ye Olde Cunzie Neuk", Thomas Young's "Masonic Arms", John Cowan's "Golden Cross Tavern", William Beaumont's "Volunteer Arms", Andrew Fleming's "West Port Hotel" and the "Palace Hotel" which described itself as "in every way suitable for visitors and commercial men", with "Cyclists' quarters, stabling and hiring."

With so many licensed grocers and inns, pubs and hotels, local chemists were no doubt often called upon to supply plenty of hangover cures. Thomas Lumsden M.P.S. 17 High Street however seems to have catered for the best of both worlds for he also stocked beer and ales as well as medicines. He also advertised "Linlithgow's aerated waters, special quality mineral waters made from the water of the famous and ancient well of the Crusaders, the Knights Templar."

Linlithgow's other chemist, C. M. Spence 133 to 135 High Street with a branch at 67 High Street at the Cross also had what would today be considered an unusual combination of goods for besides drugs and medicines their shops had stationary and newsagency departments selling "a large selection of photographic views, "The History of Linlithgow", "Guide to the Palace", "Walks round the Roman Wall" and other local publications as well as daily and weekly newspapers and periodicals. Subscribers papers punctually delivered."

Several adverts refer to drapers such as Alex. McDonald 213 High Street. "Clothier, Milliner Dress and Mantle Maker" and L. H. Ballantine 121 High Street who stated that he "always carried on hand a very large stock of Ladies' jackets, mantles and millinery of the finest choice and at the lowest cash prices."

One place where the ladies of Linlithgow might well have worn their latest hats was the Miss Drawbells' Victoria Restaurant, while Haig and Blake, Bakers and Confectioners promised home baking to "visitors and excursionists" who called at their tea room "opposite the Cross Well."

While the ladies enjoyed tea and cakes the 1900 Marches programme urged gentlemen to patronise the Victoria hairdressing saloon, "where every attention is paid to the comfort and convenience of customers" who could also purchase "cigars of choice brand, cigarettes and tobacco as well as a large assortment of pipes to select from."

For the home P. G. Fleming, Plumber and Gas Fitter could supply, "sanitary appliances on the newest and most approved principals as well as gas stoves and incandescent lights." His rivals Dymock Brothers advertised the "Acme" knife cleaner for 10/-, the " Non Pareil" wringer and mangles and promised to recover rubber rollers. They guarranteed "all rubber rollers to be of solid white rubber throughout and that the rubber will not become loose and slip on the spindle."

Another guarantee of complete satisfaction was Dentist G. Francis Gentle who although his surgery was in Falkirk offered to visit patients residing in Linlithgow or district by appointment "to fit artificial teeth mounted on gold, platinum and vulcanite."

Once fitted with new teeth Black Bitches were invited to visit W. T. Taylor's photographic parlour, "Specialities Children and Out Door

Work." No doubt Marches Day 1900 would provide him with plenty of subjects as it is to be hoped that future Marches will do his contemporary equivalents.

The Deacon's Court has expanded Marches Day into a whole week of festivities centred on a marquee erected in the grounds of the Old Academy at Low Port.

It is clear therefore that there is still plenty of life left in the old Marches and it is to be hoped they will continue without interruption for at least another 600 years.

While it is hoped that all the old traditions mentioned in the text of this booklet will be faithfully kept it is to be hoped also that new ones will be added such as the involvement of more bands and other groups from overseas. It is to be hoped too that more and more young people of the town will be encouraged to take an even greater part in the Marches. For it is from the young Black Bitches that the desire to keep the Marches alive must come and long may they wish each other "Happy Marches".

Chapter 6

Winchburgh En Fete

A touch of continental gaiety is brought to the Scottish sabbath on the final Sunday of May each year, when the Roman Catholic parishioners of Winchburgh, West Lothian's old shale mining village midway between Linlithgow and Kirkliston enjoy their annual feast day.

Winchburgh with its long low lines of red brick miners' rows, is still dominated by its vast pink plateau like shale bing, and it was the shale oil boom of Victorian times, which resulted in such a strong Catholic community as many Irish families came to take advantage of the available work. Later the building of the Forth Railway Bridge in the 1880's with its big demand for labourers attracted even more Irishmen to both Winchburgh and Kirkliston and the latter gained the nickname "Cheese Town", because it was claimed that cheese made up the basic diet of the Irish navvies.

Today the accents of the children at Winchburgh's attractive modern Holy Family Primary School is as Scottish as any of their Protestant neighbours, but it is good that they are still eager as ever to keep up the traditions of their parish and there is always tremendous excitement when the time comes to choose one of the girls from the Primary 7 senior class to be May Queen.

On the last Sunday in the month the excitement reaches its peak when in a ceremony similar to many of the Whit ceremonies in English towns, the young May Queen, dressed all in white makes her way in procession through the village to the church of St Philomena.

She is proceeded by one of the church's altar boys bearing a crucifix and he is followed by the parish priest and all the other altar boys in their surplices.

The Queen, herself, is accompanied by two of her friends as her ladies in waiting, while another of her classmates acts as crown bearer. At Winchburgh, unlike other West Lothian children's festivities, where the crown bearer is always a boy, the crown bearer is a girl and the crown she carries is one of flowers with which to adorn the smaller of St Philomena's two statues of the Virgin Mary.

The Statue of the Virgin Mary is borne high around the village of Winchburgh during the St. Philomena May Day festivities.

As is continental feast days, the highlight of the Winchburgh procession is the appearance of the church's other and larger statue of the Holy Mother, which is borne high by two of the men of the congregation, on this annual outing from the church.

The remainder of the procession is made up of all the other girl pupils of Holy Family Primary, whose colourful dresses and bouquets of spring flowers bring a splash of colour to the walk to church.

Once inside the church all of the children join in prayers to the Virgin Mary, before singing a special flower hymn, "We Crown Her With Blossoms". During the hymn the climax of the day's celebrations is reached, when the little crown bearer places the crown of flowers on the head of the smaller of the two statues of Mary, who in her blue gown overlooks the happy scene.

Soon the Holy Mother is surrounded by flowers as all of the flower girls parade around the church and lay their bouquets in special positions on the table at her feet. Then the service at an end, the boys and girls leave St Philomena's knowing that yet again they have kept alive one of the traditions of their village, which is unique in this part of Scotland.

Catherine Campbell playing the role of St. Teresa in 1952. She is now Mrs. Duncan and is a teacher at Holy Family Primary of which she was a pupil when she appeared in the May Day festivities. Along with a number of other changes the part of St. Teresa has disappeared from the present day celebrations.

Chapter 7

Ferry Fair

One of the most intriguing characters in the whole of Scotland's folk anthology is Queensferry's famous Burry Man, who parades the streets of the old burgh on the August Friday before each Ferry Fair.

Some people claim in fact that the Burry Man takes his name from the "burgh", which is his home, but it seems more likely that his title comes from the sticky green burrs of the burrdock plant with which he is covered from head to toe.

Gathering the burrs from the hedgerows around Queensferry and from the sides of the plateau like shale ash bings around the neighbouring villages of Dalmeny and the Newton, takes all of the week before the Ferry Fair, then long before dawn on the Fair Friday, The Burry Man's loyal supporters begin the lengthy task of putting on his bizarre costume.

Wearing woolen long johns and knitted gloves and balaclava helmet, the Burry Man stands with arms outstreched while the burrs are stuck all over him. When at last every burr is stuck in position the Burry Man with a head dress of flowers and two colourfully decorated flower covered staffs in his hands, is ready to walk the streets of the Ferry.

As he makes his way along the long narrow High Street with its distinctive double levelled rows of shops and houses and up the steep braes of the Loan past the distillery, the Burry Man has the right to claim a kiss from every pretty girl he encounters, while everyone else is expected to put money in his collecting cans.

The Burry Man's "walkabout" continues until dusk, thus keeping up one of Scotland's oldest traditions, but what exactly was its origin is veiled in the mists of antiquity.

One local legend is that the Burry Man was originally a shipwrecked sailor. Washed up on the south shore of the River Forth, without a scrap of clothing, he is said to have covered himself in burrs to cover his embarrassment, before venturing into Queensferry to seek help.

Much more likely explanation is that the Burry Man started as a fertility symbol, thus explaining his appearance at the start of the harvest season, the floral head dress and the bunches of flowers in his hands, as well, of course, as all those kisses.

Next day Queensferry's celebrations continue with its Ferry Fair. Today the centre piece of the festivities is the crowning of the town's school girl queen, chosen in turn from each of the town's three primary (elementary) schools, but older traditions are still maintained. These include the Burgh Race, around the boundaries of the town and the High

Street Race, with its memories of "Killiecrankie" in his scarlet uniform and his Glengarry bonnet, bearing the traditional prize of a pair of boots.

Another highlight is the fun as the local boys take it in turn to try to climb to the top of the greasy pole in the Burgess Park, with its memories of days gone by when sailors used to scale the rigging and masts of the sailing ships in Queensferry's tiny crowded harbour.

Later in the summer on 4th September, another short ceremony takes place off the shore at Queensferry, when a Royal Naval vessel makes a special crossing of the Forth to mark the official opening by Her Majesty, Queen Elizabeth on Friday 4th September 1964 of the long awaited Forth Road Bridge and the subsequent ending after nearly 900 years of the ferry passage founded by Queen Margaret, wife of Malcolm Canmore, from whom the burgh gets its name and its coat of arms.

Final ceremony every year in Queensferry, is always the switching on of the town's Christmas lights. Not only do these lights brighten the seafront with their sparkling reflection in the dark waters of the Forth as they transform the outline of the old burgh buildings into a fairy tale castle, but the Christmas tree also reminds the people of the Ferry of the war time years, when a real prince came to find freedom in their midst.

He was the dashing young Prince Olaf of Norway and along with other naval officers he came to Scotland to fight back against the Germans when they invaded his homeland in 1940. Throughout the war they supported the resistance workers in Norway and each year in December, these freedom fighters showed that they too still remembered their prince in exile across the waters by ensuring that a Christmas tree was smuggled out of Norway and across the North Sea to his base in Queensferry.

Today that custom is still maintained with the people of Norway sending a giant Christmas tree to be erected in London's Trafalgar Square and welcoming the 1981 tree, Norway's Ambassador to the United Kingdom contrasted its public reception with the war time Christmas celebrations in Queensferry, when the tree came in secret, but always arrived to provide their prince with his link with the country of which he was to become King.

74

Chapter 8

Infirmary Day Pageants

During the late 1920's and 1930's one of the highlights of the summer months, apart from the Fair, was the annual Infirmary Pageant, which in those days long before the Welfare State and the National Health Service came into existence raised thousands of pounds for the upkeep of the famous Edinburgh Hospital.

In may ways the Bo'ness Infirmary Pageants resembled student rag weeks and on may occasions the Edinburgh students did travel out to the town to help with the fund raising, but on the whole the stunts which were staged to keep up public interest were all thought of by the young people of Bo'ness. One of the most famous of these stunts was that of the Great Elk's egg. When it was at last revealed to the waiting audience it turned out to be square, so that it would not roll of the ledges where the Bo'ness naturalists claimed the bird always nested.

The most important part of the Pageant Week was the procession which each year had a different theme. One was the History of Bo'ness, and the Romans and all the other people connected with town's story were portrayed on the tableaux. Another year local industry was taken as the theme and each factory in the town was represented. A lifeboat decorated the P. & W. MacLellan lorry, while the Carriden miners had a scene on their lorry depicting shot firing with real coal and fireworks to produce realistic bangs.

Usually these pageants, under the guidance of the late Bailie Robert Baptie, raised about £400 for the Infirmary and on one proud occasion over £800 was raised. Today only a few copies of "Sine Metu", the special newspaper issued during Pageant Weeks, remain to recall these festivities of pre-war days.

Chapter 9

Hogmanay

It's Not Quite As Scottish As You May Think!

There's nothing as Scottish as Hogmanay . . . or is it?

For in fact Hogmanay is actually an old Norse word meaning the eve of the fairies — and is one last reminder that all Scotland's New Year festivities were imported by the Vikings, when they brightened the dark cold winter nights with their Yule celebrations.

In other parts of Northern Europe and even in the Scandinavian homelands of the Vikings themselves, Yule became assimilated into the spread of Christmas in the middle ages, until today even the traditional Yule log is thought of as a Christmas decoration.

Scotland alone had preserved the supernatural elements of the old Norse fairies' eve, with all of its Hogmanay superstitions about dark first foots and the gifts which they should bear.

In most parts of Scotland that's as far as the Hogmanay traditions go, but in one or two places a few other vestiges of the original Yule still survive.

At Burghead, on the Moray Firth, for instance, fire plays an important part in welcoming the New Year, not at midnight on December 31 as one might expect, but 12 days later. For as well as maintaining the old Yule customs, the townsfolk of Burghead still adhere to the old calendar, officially abandoned in 1752, which means that for them Hogmanay falls on January 11.

It is then that Burghead's age-old ceremony of the burning of the clavie will yet again take place. The clavie is a tar barrel and it is set alight with a brand of burning peat. Once it is aflame it is then carried by relays of runners round and round the streets of the old fishing port until it is finally born to the top of Dourie Hill.

There it is set down on a stone on the summit, surrounded by the crowd. After its flames have lit up the night sky with their promise of the return of the light nights of spring and summer lying ahead, the clavie is rolled back down the hill and broken into pieces, possession of one of which is regarded as a good luck symbol for the coming year.

For Scotland's other well-known fire festival, Lerwick's Up-Helly-Aa, it's necessary to wait until January 26, but Shetland's neighbouring islands, the Orkneys, re-enact their own piece of Viking lore each New Year's day, when both men's and boys' ba' games fill the narrow streets of Kirkwall with surging throngs.

With the shops barricaded to prevent smashed windows, the ba' games, which are somewhat similar to those held in Jedburgh on Candlemas Day, begin in mid-morning and rage on until dusk with the men and boys of both halves of the island town vying desperately for possession of the ball.

In Kirkwall, as in may other Scottish ports, the New Year is still often welcomed with the blowing of ships' sirens, but it's sad that the cannon which once blasted in the midnight air at Bo'ness each Hogmanay is now only a memory.

For there, as in most other Scottish towns, more and more families are content to welcome in the year gathered round their TV sets and leave the cold night air to those old Norse fairies who gave Hogmanay its name.

Chapter 10

High Days and Holidays

A hundred and even fifty years ago holidays were far, far fewer than today and therefore their enjoyment was perhaps all the greater.

Sunday school outings still take place on summer Saturdays, bus now these balloon and streamer decked but outings to Burntisland, North Berwick and Dunbar have to compete with the promise of holidays in France, Majorca or even Florida.

In the past this was not so and these outings were the highlight of the whole year. Perhaps even for today's children, they would however have had a certain excitement if not for their destinations then certainly for the variety and the style of their transport.

Many Sunday schools relied on friendly farmers to supply their big wheeled hay carts to carry crowds of children, which would horrify modern safety officers with their Health and Safety at Work manuals, but which delighted the youngsters as they clip clopped their way down to the seaside at Blackness, Society and Hopetoun.

In Linlithgow Sunday school outings were also horse powered but often instead of a hay ride, the young Black Bitches enjoyed the thrill of a canal trip, with the large coal barges specially cleaned out for the occasion. Starting out from the Manse Basin, the barges usually sailed westwards with Carriber Glen on the banks of the River Avon, below the massive Aqueduct a favourite setting for picnic and the sports, which were obligatory features of all such excursions.

While Linlithgow children sailed the waters of the Union Canal on their Sunday School trips, Bo'ness bairns ofter embarked on the River Forth's most famous paddle steamer "The Fair Maid" to voyage all the way to Burntisland, Aberdour or even Kinghorn.

As well as Sunday schools many other local organisations ranging from the Band of Hope to the staffs of big houses all organised their summer treats and two of them are captured for all time in these pictures which show the staff of Balbardie House, Bathgate and the musicans and friends of Bathgate Amateur Orchestra enjoying their days in the country.

Chapter 11

Bathgate's Newlands Day

There can be few children's days when the boys and girls remember school, but this is the case in Bathgate, where the town's annual gala day on the first Saturday each June is dedicated to John Newlands, the fouder of Bathgate Academy.

Newlands was born in Fauldhouse, but spent his boyhood years in Bathgate. From there he emigrated to Jamaica, where he made his fortune as a plantation owner. He never returned to Scotland, but he never forgot the town of his youth and when he died he left all of his considerable fortune to "erect a free school in the parish of Bathgate."

His relatives were furious and fought the will for fifteen years from Newlands' death in 1799 until 1814. The trustees appointed by Newlands to see to the building of the school, were naturally alarmed at the prospect of becoming invoved in costly legal proceedings and if it had not been for the persistence of Marjoribanks of Balbardie House they would have abondoned the suit, but in the end they received £14,500. This was only a fifth of what Newlands had intended and it took until 1831 for sufficient interest to be amassed to allow work to start on the erection of the school.

Two years later the classical Greek style Bathgate Academy, erected "on an open site to the south of the town", was ready to receive its first pupils, but although Newlands had intended their education to be free, they had to pay fees as there was not enough money left to pay the salaries of the rector and the three masters, who made up its staff.

Today the town has expanded around the school and with the expansion has come the need for a much larger comprehensive secondary school, which has been erected on the modern outskirts at Boghall. It is however to the original grey stone Academy with its distinctive facade with its columns and colonades that the crowds still flock on the eve of

Thrice around the Cross.

"Happy Marches". The crowd follows the Reed Band led by Peter Middlemas up the steep Kirk Gate to the fraternisation in the forecourt of the Palace.

82

Provost Tulloch at the fencing of the court on the steps of the Burgh Halls in 1936.

Provost Tulloch holds the Loving Cup outside the Bridge Inn, Linlithgow Bridge at the 1936 Marches.

The reading of the proclamation at the Cross.

"We Saw You First", the joiners' carriage at a Marches at the beginning of this century. Notice the continuation of the old custom of decorating both carriage and horses with long wood shavings.

84

The 1931 Royal Court at Linlithgow Gala Day.

The 1935 Gala Day Queen and Royal Court pose for the photographer outside the Old Entry in Linlithgow Palace Court Yard.

85

The local populace pose proudly in front of one of Bathgate's prize winning arches in Cochrane Street. Does the slogan "Welcome Back Again" refer to troops returning from the First World War?

The same arch in Cochrane Street as the Newlands Day Procession made its way through the town.

86

An early John Newlands Day procession makes its way east along Bathgates's South Bridge Street.

The Marjoribanks Street arch which won first prize in 1914. Note the wrong spelling of Marjoribanks. The street was in fact named after Alexander Marjoribanks the owner of Balbardie House who led the fight to establish Bathgate Academy which is the most prominent building in the street.

The Bathgate Orchestra summer outing in 1896. Notice the capacious tea urn!

A summer outing from Balbardie House, home of Alexander Marjoribanks (Back Row 1. John Addison, 4 Wm. Addison, 7 Wm. White. Kneeling — John Addison Sen. Mrs. White Sitting on mat — 1 George White. 3 Alex White, Miss Robertson, Miss Hastie, Miss Wolfe).

An unusual Newlands Day picture showing the staff of Bathgate Academy which was founded with Newlands' money.

Whitburn Gala Day in the 1920's?

Newlands Day to hear the traditional oration, with which the annual celebrations always begin.

The oration is always given by one of Bathgate Academy's many successful former pupils and it is considered the town's highest honour to be asked to give it.

Next morning all the pupils from all the schools in Bathgate join in a procession through the streets of the town, which are always colourfully

SGP
1982.

decorated with bunting and arches. Highlight of the procession is the horse drawn open landau bearing senior pupils from either the Academy or from St Mary's Academy, playing the roles of Princess Marjory, daughter of Robert the Bruce and her husband Walter the High Steward, who during the 14th century lived in Bathgate Castle, which stood on a site in the middle of what is now the town's golf course.

After the procession, which includes many impressive tableaux including those designed by the apprentices at the British Leyland Truck and Tractor Factory and by the staff and pupils at Balbarbie Primary School, the children gather at the Meadows Park for the sports and shows, which round of the big day.

Earlier in the summer in May the Meadows Park is also the scene of Bathgate's Highland Games, which although of comparatively recent

Two fine examples of the work of the arch builder from Bathgate's Gideon Street in 1915 and the town's High Street in 1910.

origins are now ranked as among the best in Scotland, with athletes, dancers and pipe bands all combining to make Games Saturday one of West Lothian's most colourful days of the year.

Following Bathgate Games every Saturday in May and June right through to the first Saturday in July sees a gala day somewhere in West Lothian, with Boghall, Blackburn, Armadale and Whitburn all following one upon the other, until the season ends with Linlithgow's children's day on the first Saturday in July.

It's appropriate that this final gala, before the children break up for the long summer holidays, takes place in such a spectacular setting on the grassy slopes of the Peel beneath the walls of Linlithgow Palace overlooking the tranquil waters of the loch, for while it is now centuries since Scotland's kings and queens chose West Lothian for their summer residence, each of the disricts modern "royal" families still bring a touch of regal dignity to the workaday world of its towns and villages on each of these gala Saturdays.

Chapter 12

When the Knights Come Home

Torphichen, nestling high in the Bathgate Hills, is famed as the medieval headquarters of the Knights of St John of Jerusalem in Scotland and on Saint John's Day, the last Sunday in June each year, the modern successors of these Knights come home.

Wearing their distinctive black robes, with their famous white eight pointed Maltese crosses and carrying their swords and banners with the insignia of their order, which claims to be the oldest order of chivalry in the world, the Knights march in procession to the ancient Preceptory.

There in the thick stone walled Preceptory, which takes its name from the Christian precepts from which the Knights derive their code of conduct, they meet in worship and recall the Orders principle vow, "to help their lords, the sick."

Later to the sounds of Torphichen and Bathgate Pipe Band, the Knights and their supporters gather for afternoon tea on the lawns of the village school.

Today the modern headquarters of the Knights of St John in Scotland is in St John Street near Moray House, just off Edinburgh's historic Royal Mile, but a branch of the Association of St John maintains its links with Torphichen and its members continue the Order's charitable work not only in the village, but throughout West Lothian with particular support for Bangour Hospital and Wallhouse Children's Home.

In addition to the annual St John's Day celebrations other items on its calendar of events include garden fetes, barn dances and at Christmas, a candle lit carol service in Torphichen Kirk.

The 18th century church is also the scene for the yearly kirkin' of Torphichen's school girl queen, which is the final event in the village's three days of gala celebrations each June.

The gala begins on the second last Friday in June with a young herald

*The Preceptory of the Knights of St. John where celebrations take place
each St. John's Day, the final Sunday in June.*

*Inside the Preceptory during the Knights of St. John exhibition. A perma-
nent display has now been mounted in the rooms above the choir.*

SGP
1982

in traditional tabard and accompanied by pipes and drums, marching down the Loan to the Diamond Jubilee Well in the village square, where he deliveres a proclamation calling on all the inhabitants to attend the festivities of the morrow. The remainder of the Friday evening is given over to decoration of the village, with particular attention being paid to the homes of the young queen and her royal court.

The following morning all of the decorated house fronts and arches are judged, while the excitement mounts still further with the judging of the children's fancy dress parade. At noon the procession round the whole of the village begins and as well as the young school girl queen, who is chosen from Torphichen lassies in their first year at Bathgate Academy and her retinue of ladies in waiting, bower girls, flower girls and fairies, it also includes many of the village boys. Four of them play the usual gala roles of champion, standard bearer, crown bearer and sceptre bearer, but

Torphichen Gala Queen Margaret Pender.

Mrs. W. Wolfe crowning the Torphichen Gala Queen.

Torphichen Gala Queen Moira Black.

Torphichen Gala Queen Wilma McCulloch.

in addition in Torphichen eight of them play the roles of the Knight of St John and very appropriately it is to them that the honour falls to provide the escort for the queen.

The procession ends in the grounds of the school, where the colourful crowning ceremony takes place. Later in the afternoon villagers, both Torphichen born and newcomers alike come together on the village green for the children's sports, the climax of which is always the village marathon, which has become one of the gala's traditions.

After an evening of festivities at the fun fair on the green, in the Torphichen Inn, in the village social club and at the gala dance in the community centre, the following Sunday morning sees all the children back in costume for the kirkin' ceremony in the church, during which the queen receives a white leather bound Bible from the parish minister.

A final procession through the village led by a piper, brings the queen back to the school and the everyday life of the village, but next year Torphichen is always ready yet again to enjoy its gala festivities.

Chapter 13

Bo'ness Opera Week

Apart from the Fair the most important event of the year in Bo'ness has always been Opera Week, in the early spring.

In March 1982 Bo'ness Amateur Operatic Society celebrated its golden jubilee performance with an especially lavish production of Franz Lehar's "Merry Widow", but the society's history stretches back even further than fifty years, because like the Fair it was reluctantly forced to miss several years because of the Great Depression and the two World Wars

It was in 1912 that the first Bo'ness "opera" was staged in the then new Town Hall which had been opened eight years earlier in the Glebe Park and apart from one occasion during the 1920's when the members of the society were tempted to try out the facilities of the Hippodrome which local architect Matthew Steel had designed in Hope Street, the Town Hall despite all its production difficulties has remained the setting for all Bo'ness Amateur Operatic Society's productions ever since.

For their first show the members of Bo'ness Opera chose Gilbert and Sulivan's "H.M.S. Pinafore" and it proved so popular and successful that in 1913 they chose the same pair's "Pirates of Penzance" with "The Mikado" following in 1914.

The First World War put an end to productions and it was not until 1922 that the company presented their next show when they decided once again to produce, "The Mikado".

From then until 1926 the society remained loyal to Gilbert and Sulivan, but in 1927 they broke new ground when they staged "Merrie England". In 1928 and 1929 however they returned to G. and S. with "Iolanthë" and "The Gondoliers" until for 1930 they voted to present a modern musical comedy with a French setting, which had proved a big success on the London West End stage, "Les Cloches de Cornevill".

Unfortunately due to the Great Depression it was the last show which they

My Mother, Peggy Snedden, behind the counter in Fraser's Chemist Shop where besides serving prescriptions she conducted the bookings for the Bo'ness "Opera".

could afford to produce for six years until in 1936 a group of young enthusiasts in Bo'ness including solicitor A. B. Simpson, J. Russell Fleming, the music teacher and organist, Fergus McLellan, who later joined the Carl Rosa Opera Company and his sister Helen McLellan afterwards infant mistress at the Grange School revived the society and staged a sparkling new production of "The Mikado". After months of rehearsal in McLellan's Hall in Corbiehall the show was a resounding success with gales of laughter from capacity audiences of 700 and 800 who even sat on the window sills of the balcony of the Town Hall.

Encouraged by their success, in 1937 with the same producer Jack Lennox they decided to be adventurous and staged Lionel Monckton's new musical "The Quaker Girl". This was Bo'ness Operatic Society at its height, long before the challenge of television, and enthusiasm in the town ran so high that when booking for the show opened in Fraser the chemist's, queues in Hope Street formed before dawn to ensure getting the best seats for the Friday and Saturday night performances.

Long before these final performances "The Quaker Girl" had proved as

The Cast of Bo'ness Opera's 1936 production of "The Mikado". Including J. Russell Fleming as Coco whose "little list" on this occasion included Fergus McLellan, Helen McLellan, Mary Murray, Chrissie Grant, Ethel Russell, George Wiggans, John Jeffrey (of Viewforth Hotel fame) and seated in front John Douglas Snedden now producer of the Bo'ness Fair Royal Command Performance and many musical shows.

triumphant a success as "The Mikado" with the whole town echoing Fergie McLellan's rendering of "Come to the Ball".

Two other popular shows "Florodora" with its hit number "Tell Me Pretty Maiden" and "A Country Girl" which sent audiences away happily singing. "The Rajah of Bhong" followed in 1938 and '39 but then war again halted productions.

"For the boys coming home we decided to start up again as quickly as possible and this we did with "Good Night Vienna" in 1947," explained Miss Helen McLellan. Miss McLellan did not take a part in "Good Night Vienna" for which she was Assistant Producer but in 1948 as well as helping with production she returned to the cast of "Geisha" and in 1949 went on to

The 1937 Bo'ness Opera production of "The Quaker Girl" with left to right Bobby Hunter, Helen McLellan, Andrew Strachan, Ena McCallum, Fergus McLellan and Chrissie Grant.

revive her success of 1939 as Madam Sofie in a new production of "A Country Girl", other leading players included Helen Burnett, Elizabeth Sneddon and Margaret Grant.

1950 brought a new show with a South American setting "Rio Rita" and there followed a succession of hits for the society with shows including "The Desert Song", "Rose Marie" and "No No Nanette".

In 1958 the society presented the American musical "Annie Get Your Gun" and this was followed by several other trans Atlantic hits including "South Pacific" with Douglas Snedden as Emile De Becque, Doris Ann Aitken as Ensign Nellie Forbush, Joe McLaren as Lieutenant Cable, Charlie Frank as Luther Billis, Myrna Saddler as Bloody Mary, Daisy Panton as Liat and society stalwart George Aitken as the Commander.

In 1961 the choice was the very Scottish "Brigadoon" which set the style for a series of successes during the 1960's including "The Student Prince",

"Oklahoma", "King's Rapsody" and the company's first production of "The Merry Widow" in 1964.

During the 1970's a succession of young Bo'nessians including George Paton, Tom and Jim Arthur, Janice Worrall, June Connor, David English and Mary Gilfillan kept up the society's high standards with productions of new shows including "The King And I" and revivals of others including "Rose Marie" and "Oklahoma".

In 1980 the company produced "My Fair Lady" with husband and wife team Hamish and Pam Duncan in the leading roles.

Thus "Opera" going in Bo'ness has developed over three quarters of a century into something of a tradition and at the golden jubilee production of "The Merry Widow" in 1982, the opening night was turned into a gala performance with the large audience seated cafe style at tables. As the champagne corks popped Society President Brian Burt paid tribute to past members such as John Miller and Sybil Muir and present members and indicated that there was promise too for the future from the number of enthusiastic youngsters already helping the company back stage and in front of the house who were waiting eagerly to take part in future "operas".

Chapter 14

Festival of Transport

Latest addition to the local festive scene is the Scottish Rail Preservation Society's "Festival of Transport".

Since establishing its headquarters on the shores of the Forth at Bo'ness, the society's Victorian style station and engine sheds have become a mecca for rail enthusiasts from all over the country, but never more so than during the weekend following Bo'ness Fair, when the town's traditional children's day celebrations are extended by two full days of events connected with the history of transport.

The Festival of Transport begins on the Saturday morning with a colourful parade through the streets of Bo'ness of all kinds of vintage and veteran vehicles. These range from cars to traction engines and from early motor cycles to steam rollers, while the ancient buses always bring back memories of by-gone outings to many of the older people in the crowds which always turn out to see the procession.

The parade is followed by arena events and other static displays around the platforms of the old station, which originally stood at Wormit at the Fife end of the Tay Bridge and which has been carefully reconstructed on the site at East Pier Street, but the undoubted stars of both days of festivities are unquestionably the Rail Preservation Society's own puffing panting and highly polished locomotives, which are all under steam for the occasion.

Star of the 1982 festival was the Swedish locomotive 1313. Built in 1919 for mixed passenger and greight haulage 1313 plied on Sweden's extensive rail network until 1963 when it was withdrawn from service and laid up. Despite its rather unlucky sounding number 1313 was eventually rescued in 1981 when it was purchased by one of the Scottish Rail Preservation Society's supporters and shipped across the North Sea to add a new international dimension to the society's collection at Bo'ness.

Dry land sailors cruise through the streets of Bo'ness.

Another well travelled locomotive is the Scottish Rail Preservation Society's pride and joy, Caledonian Railway Suburban tank engine 419, which spent the summer of 1982 as the guest of England's famous and much televised and filmed Blue Bell Line where 419's immaculate light blue livery was particularly appropriate.

At present the Scottish Railway Preservation Society's collection of engines is still divided between its new headquarters at Bo'ness and its marshalling yard at Grahamston, Falkirk, but as soon as the society's eventual aim to re-open the whole of the Bo'ness to Manuel single track branch line is achieved, hopefully in about five years, all of the locomotives including the L.N.E.R. mainline "Morayshire" which at present operates very popular steam excursions to many parts of Scotland and England over British Rail truck, will be transferred to Bo'ness.

Then in addition to operating a regular service from Bo'ness along the banks of the Forth to Kinneil Halt then on through the woods to Birkhill and Todd's Mill where there will be a picnic site and eventually on to

Manuel Junction and Polmont, the society looks forward to many of its locomotives including the gleaming black painted North British 060 "Maude" running special excursions, thus reviving an important part of the Bo'ness social scene of past years.

It is in fact interesting to note that the very first passenger train to operate from the original Bo'ness Station at the foot of the Wynd in Corbiehall was an excursion special chartered for the day by the owners of the local potteries to provide their employees with their first ever organised outing.

So far only half a mile of track of the Scottish Railway Preservation Society's Bo'ness and Kinneil Railway is operational, but already the sounds and sights of the steam trains are bringing back many memories to the town's older inhabitants, as regular trips along the shore past the old docks and harbour, which it is also planned to turn into a maritime steam museum, are operated on most Saturdays and Sundays.

Rolling stock is as varied as the society's collection of engines and includes a L.N.E.R. suburban compartment carriage and a buffet car which will soon once more be ready to serve refreshments, but the new railway's pride and joy is the royal carriage in which King Edward VII travelled along Royal Deeside from Aberdeen to his castle at Balmoral.

The Scottish Rail Preservation Society has not so far been honoured with a royal visit, but on the weekends before Christmas it always looks forward to carrying a V.I.P., Very Important Passenger, as its Santa Specials have become great favourites with children from Bo'ness and all parts of Forth Country.